MARTIN LUTHER KING JR.
FIGHTING FOR CIVIL RIGHTS

Neil Armstrong

Jackie Robinson

Harriet Tubman

Jane Goodall

Albert Einstein

Beyoncé

Stephen Hawking

Simone Biles

Martin Luther King Jr.

J. K. Rowling

»TRAIL BLAZERS

MARTIN LUTHER KING JR.
FIGHTING FOR CIVIL RIGHTS

CHRISTINE PLATT

RANDOM HOUSE 🏠 NEW YORK

Text copyright © 2020 by Christine Platt
Cover art copyright © 2020 by Luisa Uribe
Interior illustrations copyright © 2020 by David Shephard

All rights reserved. Published in the United States by Random House Children's Books, a division of Penguin Random House LLC, New York.

Random House and the colophon are registered trademarks of Penguin Random House LLC.

Visit us on the Web! rhcbooks.com

Educators and librarians, for a variety of teaching tools, visit us at RHTeachersLibrarians.com

Library of Congress Cataloging-in-Publication Data is available upon request.
ISBN 978-0-593-12455-0 (trade pbk.)— ISBN 978-0-593-12456-7 (lib. bdg.)— ISBN 978-0-593-12457-4 (ebook)

Created by Stripes Publishing Limited, an imprint of the Little Tiger Group

Printed in the United States of America

First Edition

Random House Children's Books supports the First Amendment and celebrates the right to read.

Penguin Random House LLC supports copyright. Copyright fuels creativity, encourages diverse voices, promotes free speech, and creates a vibrant culture. Thank you for buying an authorized edition of this book and for complying with copyright laws by not reproducing, scanning, or distributing any part in any form without permission. You are supporting writers and allowing Penguin Random House to publish books for every reader.

Contents

Introduction — 1
Martin's Dream

Chapter 1 — 17
A Leader Is Born

Chapter 2 — 31
Young Man on a Mission

Chapter 3 — 53
Boycotting Segregation

Chapter 4 — 73
A Movement Begins

Chapter 5 — 89
The Fight for Civil Rights

Chapter 6 — 105
The March on Washington

Chapter 7 — 121
A New America

Conclusion — 143
An American Hero

Timeline — 152

Further Reading — 158

Glossary — 160

Index — 164

INTRODUCTION

MARTIN'S DREAM

On August 28, 1963, Martin Luther King Jr. climbed the steps of the Lincoln Memorial in Washington, DC, and delivered a speech to hundreds of thousands of people about a dream he had. Standing in front of the vast crowd, Martin told them that he dreamed of a world in which all people were treated equally and where racism didn't exist.

Martin was speaking at the March on Washington for Jobs and Freedom, a peaceful protest organized by civil rights groups to bring attention to the fight for equality. Martin's "I Have a Dream" speech would go on to become one of the most powerful speeches of the civil rights movement. It sparked something in those who heard it and pushed them to demand further action to address inequality between white and black people in America, and it put pressure on the government to make a change.

But this iconic speech almost didn't take place. On the night before the march, as Martin sat in his hotel room preparing, one of his friends, Reverend Wyatt Tee Walker, gave him some advice. Wyatt told Martin that he didn't think it was a good idea to use a speech people had already heard. Martin had recited a version of the "I Have a Dream" speech at an event in Detroit, Michigan, just two months before. So Martin wrote a new speech called "Normalcy—Never Again." He stayed up all night with his advisors to work on it. They didn't finish writing until 3:30 a.m.!

As the public speeches began, people gathered to hear leaders of the movement demand equal civil rights for black and white American citizens. Martin was the last speaker to take the stage. Walking to the podium, Martin hoped the crowd would embrace his new speech as a call to action. But as he was speaking, Mahalia Jackson, who was known as the Queen of Gospel and was one of Martin's favorite singers, called out to him, "Tell 'em about the dream, Martin! Tell 'em about the dream!"

Mahalia had heard "I Have a Dream" before. She had met Martin years earlier at one of his protests and had followed his career closely ever since.

Martin paused, put his notes aside, and then said, "I still have a dream...." Instead of continuing his planned speech, Martin went on to deliver "I Have a Dream."

Throughout his life, Martin organized many marches like the March on Washington, where he gave similar speeches about civil rights. At the time, much of America was segregated, which meant that black and white citizens lived, worked, and socialized separately. Even though the Declaration of Independence says "all men are created equal," the reality was totally different. Martin's dedication to the cause of equality, and his skill at making speeches, made him a key part of the civil rights movement, which was a push to end segregation so that everyone had the same rights. He believed that all US citizens deserve to be able to vote, to be paid a fair wage, and to go to public places, regardless of their race.

SLAVERY IN AMERICA

Racism in the United States goes back a long way and has its roots in the system of slavery. When European settlers were setting up the first colonies of America, they employed their fellow white men and women as indentured servants—people who would work for a set number of years in exchange for fare to America, housing, and food. The first Africans arrived in Jamestown, Virginia, in 1619, on the *White Lion*. Because there weren't yet any slave laws in the new colonies, these Africans were treated as indentured servants, too. But soon there was a change in their status and rights. White people considered dark skin a sign of inferiority. New laws were put in place that differentiated between white indentured servants and black enslaved people. As the colonies and the need for labor grew, landowners moved away from a system of indentured servitude and turned to the African slave trade as a cheaper, more convenient way to get laborers.

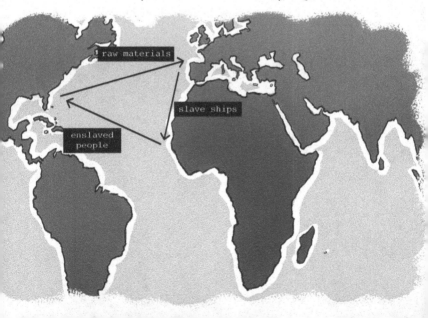

Millions of men, women, and children were kidnapped from West and Central Africa, transported across the Atlantic to the Americas, and sold into slavery. Some of the captives were forced to labor in the fields on large plantations, planting and harvesting crops such as tobacco, rice, cotton, and sugarcane. Others were made to work as carpenters, blacksmiths, shoemakers, or weavers. Some enslaved women were housekeepers and were required to cook, clean, and take care of the slaveholders' children.

In addition to being forced to work without pay, enslaved people were often abused. Many died because of the hard work and bad conditions. Some attempted to rebel, but they were punished so harshly that most enslaved people didn't try.

But many people in America did not agree with the system of slavery. These people were called abolitionists or sympathizers because they wanted to abolish laws that said a person could own another. As a result, by 1804, all the Northern states had voted to end slavery. But in the South, where landowners used enslaved people to tend their crops, slavery remained legal. There were white abolitionists in Southern slaveholding states, too, but when they spoke up, they were branded as traitors, imprisoned, or worse. So rather than fight to change the law, some sympathizers helped runaways escape slavery by fleeing to the North using secret routes such as the Underground Railroad.

The Underground Railroad

The Underground Railroad was a network of people who helped runaways escape slavery in the South and reach one of the free Northern states or Canada. The system consisted of secret routes and places to hide, including churches, barns, and safe houses, many of which were owned by sympathetic white people.

When America's Civil War began on April 12, 1861, the Northern states formed the Union army and Southern states formed the Confederate army. Many formerly enslaved black soldiers served in the Union army to help the North defeat the South. President Abraham Lincoln, who led the Union army, thought slavery was wrong, and he issued the Emancipation Proclamation on September 22, 1862, in the hope of ending the war.

The order, which came into effect on January 1, 1863, granted freed status to any enslaved person who had escaped the Confederate South—over three million people. As soon as they crossed the border into Union territory, they became free.

By the time the major fighting ended in April 1865, more than six hundred thousand soldiers had died, including forty thousand black soldiers. The Union army's defeat of the Confederate army led to the Thirteenth Amendment to the United States Constitution. When ratified on December 6, 1865, this amendment put an end to slavery in the remaining Southern slaveholding states.

AMERICA POST-SLAVERY

Once slavery had been abolished, America faced a new problem. There were now millions of freed black people with no jobs or places to live. Most were illiterate, having been forbidden to learn how to read and write. Few had any knowledge about their African origins—America was the only home they knew.

And although they were now free, they hadn't yet been granted citizenship in the United States. Nevertheless, these formerly enslaved people considered themselves Americans, and they wanted the same rights that other citizens had. They wanted the right to buy land. They wanted to travel freely throughout the country without worrying about being attacked or imprisoned. Most of all, they wanted the right to vote.

But many white people did not consider black people their equals. Southern white lawmakers had a lot of power. They used their influence to create new laws, known as Black Codes, to control what black people could and couldn't do. Black Codes determined where black people could buy land, where they could travel, when they could go out during the day, and what time they had to be indoors at night. Many states' Black Codes also restricted the types of work that black people could do, and their pay was much less than that of white employees.

Whenever a white person claimed that a black person had violated one of the Black Codes, the accused was arrested and fined and faced punishment. Most often, the punishment was forced labor without pay.

Despite the 1868 passage of the Fourteenth Amendment to the Constitution, which granted citizenship to former slaves, and the Fifteenth Amendment in 1870, which gave black men the right to vote, black people were still not treated as equals by many white citizens, especially in states that had been part of the Confederacy. Throughout the 1870s and 1880s, Southern states and local governments passed additional laws to keep black and white people separate. Known as Jim Crow laws, they were even stricter than Black Codes. They ensured the segregation of white and black people in public spaces, such as at schools and theaters, on buses and trains, and in restrooms and restaurants.

Who Was Jim Crow?

Jim Crow was a fictional black character played by white men in performances called minstrel shows. The name comes from a folk song that was once popular among black slaves. The white performers painted their faces black and portrayed Jim Crow as clumsy and ignorant, based on racist stereotypes about black people. Wearing blackface as a costume is now considered racist and offensive.

The white people who enforced Jim Crow laws made sure that white people were the ones who had access to the best, most up-to-date facilities. Soon black people started to challenge segregation as unfair, and the matter made its way to the US Supreme Court—the highest court in the United States—with the case of *Plessy v. Ferguson*.

Homer Plessy was a mixed-race man, and his skin was so light that he often attempted to challenge

Louisiana's segregation laws by passing as a white person. On June 7, 1892, Homer purchased a first-class train ticket, but the New Orleans railroad company had been warned that he might try to sit in the whites-only railroad car. When Homer was asked to move to the blacks-only railroad car, he refused and was arrested. Homer's lawyers argued that the train's segregation law was unconstitutional under the Thirteenth and Fourteenth Amendments because black passengers did not receive equal treatment. At his first trial, Homer lost and was ordered to pay a twenty-five-dollar fine. But he continued to appeal until his case was brought before the US Supreme Court.

On May 18, 1896, the Supreme Court ruled to uphold the train's segregation law as constitutional. And on that day, racial segregation became valid and legal under a doctrine known as "separate but equal." This meant that as long as white people and black people were provided with equal facilities, it was fine to keep them separate because there was no discrimination. This court decision would result in black and white people continuing to live in a segregated America for years to come.

What's in a Name?

For a long time, racial classifications were used to separate black people from whites. When slavery was legal, a black person was either free or a slave. After the abolition of slavery, terms like *colored* and *Negro* were used to mark black people as different. In modern-day America, people of African ancestry might call themselves *black*, *African American*, *people of color*, or some other name. How a person identifies is a personal choice.

⋛ A SEGREGATED AMERICA ⋚

In the early twentieth century, segregation continued to divide society and worsen race relations. By the 1920s, it was not uncommon for white people to commit crimes against black people, including public executions known as lynchings and setting fire to the homes and businesses in black communities. While some of these incidents were isolated attacks, many of them occurred when white people joined together to form hate groups. White police officers would often turn a blind eye or, worse, take part in the violence themselves.

One of the worst incidents of racial violence happened in Tulsa, Oklahoma, when an entire black community was destroyed.

The Tulsa Race Massacre

Tulsa was once home to a thriving black community known as the Greenwood District. It was full of beautiful homes, hotels, movie theaters, and restaurants. But on May 31, 1921, everything changed. A department store clerk heard Sarah Page, the young white elevator operator for the store, scream, and then moments later saw Dick Rowland, a nineteen-year-old black teenager, running from the building. Believing that Dick must have hurt Sarah, the clerk called the police, but Sarah did not say what happened, nor did she want to press charges. Nonetheless, a rumor started to spread through Tulsa that Dick had assaulted Sarah. Angered by this, white mobs attacked the Greenwood District community, and in less than 24 hours, it was burned to the ground. It is estimated that 100 to 300 black people were killed during the violence.

A NEW AMERICA

By the time Martin Luther King Jr. was born in the late 1920s, many people had hopes that America would leave its violent and racist past behind and become a country of equal opportunity for everyone. Martin would grow up to be one of the trailblazers who helped bring those dreams closer to reality.

CHAPTER 1

A LEADER IS BORN

Martin Luther King Jr. was the son of Reverend Martin Luther King Sr. and Alberta Williams King. Reverend King was the leader of the Ebenezer Baptist Church in Atlanta, Georgia, and was a key figure in the early civil rights movement. Alberta was an educated woman who had worked as a schoolteacher until she was married in 1926. Her school district did not allow married women to teach. The Kings' first child, a daughter named Willie Christine, was born on September 11, 1927.

Martin Jr. was born on January 15, 1929, in Atlanta. As many children were in those days, Martin was born at home. A little over a year later, his younger brother, Alfred Daniel, was born on July 30, 1930, the same year Martin Luther King Sr. graduated from Morehouse College with his sociology degree. The youngest King sibling was often called by his nickname, A. D., which was also his maternal grandfather's nickname.

THE KING FAMILY

The King family lived in a popular, all-black neighborhood known as Sweet Auburn. Nestled on a tree-lined street, their two-story house was located at 501 Auburn Avenue. The home belonged to Martin's maternal grandparents, Reverend Adam Daniel Williams and Jennie Celeste Parks Williams, who also lived there.

Sweet Auburn

Sweet Auburn was one of Atlanta's prominent suburbs for middle-class black families, with many doctors and teachers among them. It also had several black-owned businesses and churches and boasted many notable firsts, including the first black-owned and -operated radio station, WERD. In 1956, *Fortune* magazine named Auburn Avenue "the richest Negro street in the world." But to Martin, Sweet Auburn was always just home.

Martin spent countless sunny afternoons playing baseball, football, and games of tag with his siblings and their friends.

Martin's father was a traditional black Baptist minister—he was very strict. If Martin and his siblings disobeyed him or got into trouble, Reverend King would punish them. Although Martin's mother helped balance the household with her sweet and gentle disposition, it was his grandmother Jennie who brought Martin the most comfort. Grandma Jennie had twelve siblings. Perhaps that was how she learned to be so patient! And even though grandparents aren't supposed to have favorites, Martin secretly believed that he was hers.

⋛ THE KING CHILDREN ⋚

Martin and his siblings were very close. He looked up to his big sister, Christine, and he enjoyed teaching his little brother, A. D., new things. Because the three siblings were so close in age, they did almost everything together.

As Martin and his siblings grew older, they shared a love for their mother's music—Alberta was a very talented musician. As soon as her children were old enough, Alberta taught them to read music notes and gave them piano lessons. One of Martin's favorite childhood pastimes was playing the piano with his mother and singing with Christine and A. D.

⋛ A LOVE OF LEARNING ⋚

As a former schoolteacher, Alberta believed in the power of education, and she taught her children how to read at an early age. Martin loved the reading, writing, and math lessons he received from his mother. By the time he was five years old, Martin was so smart that his parents decided to enroll him at Yonge Street Elementary School.

Children who lived in Atlanta needed to be six years old when they started school, but Martin was so bright that everyone thought he was the same age as his classmates—until one day when Martin's teacher overheard him talking to his friends about his last birthday party.

When Martin's teacher discovered his real age, he had to sit out the rest of the school year and return when he was six years old.

RACISM AND CHILDREN

Even as a child, Martin quickly noticed that white people were treated differently than black people. Whenever his family left the tight-knit community of Sweet Auburn, Martin saw just how mean white people were to black people. In downtown Atlanta, there were even certain stores that Martin's family wasn't allowed in.

Martin knew that segregation existed, but it was difficult for him to understand why. He didn't care that people had different skin colors. Like most children, he just wanted to play and have fun. In fact, when he was five years old, one of Martin's best friends was a white boy.

Because of segregation laws, Martin's friend lived in an all-white neighborhood, but his family owned a store in Sweet Auburn, so the two boys often played together. When they started school at six years old, they went to different schools. Martin's elementary school was all-black and his best friend's school was all-white.

From then on, whenever Martin saw his friend and tried to play games with him, the boy refused. Believing that he might have accidentally done something to upset his friend, Martin asked him why he no longer wanted to play. That's when Martin learned the truth. The boy's father didn't want them to play together ever again for one reason only—Martin was black.

Martin could not believe he had lost a friend because of his skin color, something he had no control over. He asked his mother why. Alberta then had to explain the history of slavery, segregation, and racism to her six-year-old son.

Martin always remembered that conversation. As an adult, Martin would share how much his childhood experiences with racism still hurt and troubled him.

After half a year at Yonge Street Elementary, Martin was advanced to the second grade. At age eight, his parents enrolled him at David T. Howard Colored Elementary School to continue his studies.

Even though Martin grew up in a loving home with his parents and siblings, his childhood in the segregated South wasn't easy. As Martin grew older, he began to notice and experience more racism.

Once, while shopping, Martin's family sat in seats at the front of a shoe store. A white clerk insisted they would have to move to the back seats before she could help them. But Martin's father refused. "We'll either buy shoes sitting here or we won't buy shoes at all," he told the clerk. Rather than argue or go to the back of the store, the King family left altogether. Martin was very angry that his family was treated that way simply because they were black. But he was inspired by his father's resistance to the way he was treated.

"I don't care how long I have to live with this system, I will never accept it." —Martin Luther King Sr.

LIFE IN THE MINISTRY

Martin came from a long line of Baptist preachers. His father, his grandfather, and even his great-grandfather were preachers and devoted their lives to the ministry. Martin's father was the head minister at Ebenezer Baptist Church. Being involved in church activities was an important part of King family life: Reverend King preached sermons and taught Bible study, Alberta played the organ and sang in the church choir, and Martin and his siblings helped with church duties.

As Martin grew older, he discovered that he enjoyed singing with his mother in the choir. Outside of church, too, Martin loved to perform. When he was only ten years old, Martin graced the stage at Atlanta's historic Loew's Grand Theatre to sing at the premiere of *Gone with the Wind*. Martin had such a beautiful voice, some people believed he would grow up to be a professional singer.

But like most children, Martin changed his mind several times about what he wanted to become. As a young boy, he wanted to be a firefighter. Then he dreamed of being a doctor so he could help the sick and injured. Later, as he became more aware of the challenges facing black people, Martin planned to work as an attorney so he could change discriminatory laws. But he would end up pursuing none of these aspirations. Instead Martin was destined to become a leader.

FROM MICHAEL TO MARTIN

Martin was named after his father, Reverend Martin Luther King Sr., but both Martin Jr. and his father were originally named Michael. In the summer of 1934, Reverend King went to Berlin, Germany, to attend a church meeting with other ministers from all over the world. During this trip, he learned about a holy man named Martin Luther.

Martin Luther

Martin Luther is known as the man who sparked one of the biggest religious movements in Christianity's history—the Protestant Reformation.

Born November 10, 1483, in Germany, Martin Luther studied theology and served as a priest and a monk. After reading the Bible, Martin discovered that the Roman Catholic Church's practices didn't always match what the Bible said. In fact, he found 95 such instances, and on October 31, 1517, Martin posted these to a church door for everyone to see and debate. His actions were considered revolutionary at the time; speaking out against the church was a crime. But many people agreed with him, and they decided to form new churches.

When Reverend King returned to Atlanta, he told Alberta how inspired he was by Martin Luther—so inspired that Reverend King decided to change his name in Martin Luther's honor. And because Reverend King's son was a junior, he changed his name as well.

STUDENT AND SCHOLAR

When Martin was twelve years old, his beloved grandmother Jennie Celeste Parks Williams died, and the family bought a house in another Atlanta neighborhood. Although Martin was sad to leave his childhood home, he enjoyed the move because it gave him new opportunities. He got a job as a paperboy, delivering the *Atlanta Journal*.

In September 1940, Martin began seventh grade at Atlanta University Laboratory School. After spending half a year in the eighth grade, Martin was advanced to ninth grade, which made him eligible to start high school early. By the time Martin enrolled in tenth grade at Booker T. Washington High School, he was well known throughout the community as an academic scholar. His favorite subject was English—because he loved reading.

Martin also got involved in extracurricular activities. One of his favorite pastimes was participating on his school's debate team. Martin loved public speaking, and he was admired for his oratory skills.

Segregation in Public Schools

Booker T. Washington High School was for black students only. The "separate but equal" doctrine meant that schools were allowed to be segregated as long as their facilities were equivalent. But this was often not the case. Jim Crow states spent three times as much on each white student as they did on every black student. As such, schools that black students attended were run-down, and students were taught from outdated books. Teachers in black schools earned just 60 percent of a white teacher's salary, and their training was so poor that they were often teaching students in grades above their own knowledge.

⇃ UNFAIR AND UNEQUAL ⇃

As a teenager, one of Martin's biggest frustrations involved traveling on public transportation. If there weren't enough seats for white passengers, the black passengers would have to give up their seats and stand. And that was exactly what happened one day when Martin was riding a bus home from a speech competition in Dublin, Georgia.

Martin was particularly excited because he'd won the competition, speaking on the subject of "The Negro and the Constitution." While Martin and his teacher were discussing the debate, two white passengers boarded. The bus driver interrupted Martin's conversation and told him to give up his seat for one of the white passengers. Humiliated, Martin had to stand for the rest of the ride home. It was the angriest he'd ever been in his life.

CHAPTER 2

YOUNG MAN ON A MISSION

Martin's parents believed that higher education was important, so Martin knew that he would go to college. In 1944, after he graduated from high school early, at age fifteen, Martin began his studies at Morehouse College, in Atlanta. Just as it was then, Morehouse remains the only historically black men's college.

Historically Black Colleges

Historically black colleges and universities, also known as HBCUs, were established to help formerly enslaved people and their descendants earn college degrees. Currently there are over 100 active historically black colleges and universities. Today students of all races and nationalities attend these schools.

Martin's father had graduated from Morehouse in 1930, and Martin's maternal grandfather, A. D. Williams, had also received a degree from Morehouse. Attending college was a very big achievement for black families—education was something that had been withheld from them during slavery. So Martin knew it was a great honor to continue his studies, both for himself and for his community.

Martin enjoyed the many classes that were offered at Morehouse. He liked that he was able to take subjects that weren't offered in high school, such as medicine and law, which were two career paths he considered. But Martin ultimately decided to earn a degree in sociology—the study of social relations and culture. The Sociology Department chair, Dr. Walter R. Chivers, helped Martin understand that segregation was a social problem. Martin would later become the president of the school's sociology club.

Martin joined several other on-campus clubs and activities, too. He became a member of the student council and helped represent his classmates if they had concerns on campus. Martin also joined the debate team, sang in the school's glee club, and served in the ministers' union.

Through participating in Morehouse's clubs and activities, Martin met other students with similar interests. After studying, Martin and his friends spent much of their free time together playing sports. Even though he was short, Martin played a lot of basketball. His friends often teased him for loving to dribble the ball rather than shoot it.

During his freshman year, Martin read Henry David Thoreau's essay "Civil Disobedience." Martin was moved by the author's bold decision to refuse to pay his taxes and be sentenced to jail rather than support a war he didn't agree with. Martin would later note that Thoreau's essay was his first introduction to nonviolent resistance.

In August 1946, after his sophomore year at Morehouse, Martin would write his first of many letters advocating for black people to receive equal rights. Earlier in the summer, the *Atlanta Constitution* had published two stories that deeply affected Martin. The first, printed on July 26, 1946, covered the murder of a black man named Maceo Snipes, who had been shot dead by four white men after being the only black person to vote in his district. The next day, the newspaper reported that two black couples driving near Monroe, Georgia, had been stopped by twenty white men and shot. Monroe was less than an hour's drive from Atlanta. Surely these incidents were on Martin's mind when he wrote to the *Atlanta Constitution*'s editor that black people wanted and were entitled to "the basic rights and opportunities of American citizens."

⋛ YOUNG BLACK LEADERS ⋚

Like Martin, his classmates wanted to change the world and break stereotypes about black people. And many of Martin's friends would one day have extraordinary careers and achievements.

→ **Charles Vert Willie** would become the first African American professor at Syracuse University and then be named a professor emeritus at Harvard University.

→ **Samuel DuBois Cook** would become the first black man to receive tenure at a prestigious white Southern university, Duke University, and would later serve as the president of Dillard University for 22 years.

→ **William E. Finlayson** would become a respected medical doctor and help establish Milwaukee's first black-owned bank, the North Milwaukee State Bank.

For Martin and his friends, studying at Morehouse College was more than just receiving an education. It was their introduction to the wider world and an opportunity to make a change.

⋛ A FRIEND AND MENTOR ⋛

Morehouse president Benjamin E. Mays was a big influence in the lives of his students. President Mays gave morning sermons once a week in the school's chapel, where he encouraged and challenged the young men to be upstanding citizens. He also gave them practical advice, and many Morehouse students considered President Mays a father figure. Martin often went to President Mays's office after these lectures, and the two men would discuss the ministry as well as any newsworthy events.

Benjamin E. Mays

Benjamin Elijah Mays was Morehouse College's sixth president. He was born on August 1, 1894, in a little town in South Carolina. His parents were born into slavery but later gained their freedom.

Benjamin was influenced by black leaders like Frederick Douglass and Booker T. Washington. When he visited Mysore, India, in the late 1930s, he met with Mohandas Gandhi. The two men spoke at length about nonviolent protests, and Benjamin went away inspired by their conversation.

Throughout his life, Benjamin served as a Baptist minister, a civil rights leader, and, most notably, the president of Morehouse College for almost 30 years.

Mohandas Gandhi

Mohandas Gandhi was an Indian lawyer and activist who was famous for his nonviolent approach to demanding political and social change. Born October 2, 1869, in Porbandar, India, Gandhi became known as Mahatma, or "Great Soul." He led the movement to end the long-standing British rule in India. One of his most famous peaceful protests was the Salt March of 1930, when he led a group of protesters on a 24-day march to protest the effect that the British salt tax had on poor people.

Martin was often very moved by President Mays's morning sermons. When Martin wrote for Morehouse's student newspaper, the *Maroon Tiger*, his writing reflected some of the lessons he'd learned from President Mays. In one article, Martin wrote: "We must remember that intelligence is not enough. Intelligence plus character—that is the goal of true education."

Over time, President Mays became one of Martin's most trusted mentors. He believed Martin had the makings of a great leader and wanted to help plan his future. He was the first person to introduce Martin to Gandhi's teachings on nonviolent protest.

ENTERING THE MINISTRY

Although many men in Martin's family were ministers, he wasn't sure if he wanted to follow in their footsteps. He loved church and enjoyed the music ministry, but that didn't necessarily mean he should be a preacher. He also felt a strong desire to advocate for equal rights. So Martin continued to study different subjects at Morehouse in the hope of finding his life's purpose.

Martin often shared his thoughts with his mentor, and President Mays advised Martin that there were many ways a person could bring about change—and one of those ways was by serving in the ministry. For centuries, black people had relied on their faith to help them in difficult times. And that's what Martin wanted to do—help people.

CROZER THEOLOGICAL SEMINARY

Ultimately, when Martin graduated from Morehouse in 1948, he decided to attend a seminary, an institution that teaches students how to work as ministers, priests, or rabbis. He enrolled at Crozer Theological Seminary in Chester, Pennsylvania. It would be Martin's first time away from his family in Atlanta. And it would be the first time he would attend a school with white students.

Pennsylvania was one of the first states to free enslaved people, in 1780—almost a hundred years before slavery was legally abolished in 1865. In fact, Pennsylvania had been considered a haven for black runaways looking to escape slavery in the years before the Civil War. Many cities in Pennsylvania were often the last stops along the Underground Railroad.

By the time Martin enrolled at Crozer Theological

Seminary, there were already several well-established black communities in Pennsylvania. A King family friend named Reverend J. Pius Barbour lived there. Reverend Barbour was the pastor of Calvary Baptist Church. Like Martin, he had attended Morehouse College and continued his studies at Crozer. In fact, Reverend Barbour had been the first black student to graduate from Crozer. He often invited Martin to have dinner with his family. In time, Martin began serving as student pastor at Calvary Baptist Church.

MARTIN'S INSECURITIES

Many people might think that attending a racially integrated school would be exciting for Martin. But it was an anxious time for him, at least at first. Martin was one of only eleven black students on campus. And he was very uncertain about how his white classmates would treat him.

Martin had a lot of bad memories from growing up in the segregated city of Atlanta. He remembered losing his first best friend simply because they were different races, he remembered how his family had been treated at the shoe store, and he remembered when he had

had to give up his seat on the bus to a white passenger. Martin was afraid that he would experience similar types of racism at Crozer.

During his first semester, he worried about what his classmates thought of him. Did they think he belonged at Crozer? What were their opinions on white and black students learning together? Did they see Martin as their equal?

Martin knew that some white people thought very negatively about his race. They often said that black people were always late, loud, and laughing and that their appearance was unkempt. In illustrations, white artists drew black people wearing wrinkled, stained, or patched clothing and portrayed their hair as wild and uncombed. To distance himself from these stereotypes, Martin made sure to always arrive promptly to class. On the very rare occasions when he was a minute or two late, Martin spent the rest of the lesson worrying that everyone had noticed.

I had a tendency to overdress, to keep my room spotless, my shoes perfectly shined, and my clothes immaculately pressed.

Even though Reverend Barbour took Martin under his wing, Martin missed his family very much. Christine was now attending graduate school at Columbia University in New York, and Martin missed talking to his older sister and asking her for advice. He especially missed his mother and wrote to her often. In his letters, Martin told his mother about his studies or if he'd had fun visiting with friends. And once a week, Martin's mother mailed him a letter back. Inside she would include five dollars of spending money, which would be equivalent to about fifty dollars today.

Sunday night, 10:30

Dear Mother,

Your letter was received this morning. I often tell the boys around the campus I have the best mother in the world. You will never know how I appreciate the many kind things you and daddy are doing for me. . . .

You stated that my letters aren't newsey enough. Well I don't have much news. I never go anywhere much but in these books. Some times the professor comes in class and tells us to read our assignments in Hebrew, and that is really hard.

Well I guess I must go back to studying. Give everybody my Regards.

Your son, M. L.

I eat dinner at Barbour's home quite often. He is full of fun, and he has one of the best minds of anybody I have ever met.

I am going to write a letter to the entire church next week. It should be there by the first Sunday.

Soon Martin discovered that his fears about attending Crozer were unnecessary. The white students treated Martin as their equal from the day he arrived. And by his junior year, his classmates thought so highly of Martin that he was voted class president.

As Martin's fears eased, he became a more confident student at Crozer. He focused less on what his white classmates thought about him and more on his studies. Along with the traditional teachings of famous philosophers like Aristotle and Plato, Martin read many religious works and learned about devout teachers, including his namesake, Martin Luther.

When President Mays had told Martin about Gandhi's teachings years before, Martin hadn't been sure he agreed with the Indian leader's approach. He didn't understand how love and nonviolent protests could help bring about change. Because struggles over segregation and equality often turned violent in the South, Martin believed black people should be prepared to fight back. But in 1950, Martin took a trip to Philadelphia that would serve as his inspiration for the best way to bring about social change.

⋛ LIFE LESSONS ON GANDHI ⋚

Dr. Mordecai Johnson was the president of Howard University, a historically black university located in Washington, DC, and one Sunday in 1950, he was the guest pastor at the Fellowship House of Philadelphia in Pennsylvania. Dr. Johnson had just returned from a trip to India, where he'd learned about Mohandas Gandhi's life and teachings. Excited to share what he'd learned, Dr. Johnson spoke at length about Gandhi's ability to bring about social change through nonviolent protests.

Martin had traveled to Philadelphia to hear Dr. Johnson speak and was moved by the pastor's sermon. After Martin left the Fellowship House that day, one of the first things he did was buy a half dozen books so he could learn more about Gandhi.

Gandhi believed in using a passive form of resistance called "satyagraha." In Sanskrit, *satya* means "truth" and *āgraha* means "persistence," so *satyagraha* means "truth persistence." Martin thought this was similar to the message from Jesus in the Bible to "love your enemies and pray for those who persecute you." Martin realized that it was possible to resist evil without resorting to violence when opposing those who commit evil. He wanted to use love and truth as a means of peaceful resistance in his ministry to help end segregation.

Martin graduated from Crozer Theological Seminary in 1951 as class valedictorian. He then enrolled at Boston University in Massachusetts to further his theology studies.

LIFE IN BOSTON

Unlike the segregated South, Boston was a very diverse city with people from many different races, nationalities, and religions. The city also had a vibrant college scene. There were several colleges and universities in the area, and students from various schools often hung out together. Martin really enjoyed living there and meeting people from all over the country.

Howard Thurman was the dean of Boston University's Marsh Chapel, and Martin admired his spiritual teachings and sermons. In time, Dean Thurman would become another of Martin's trusted mentors. Dean Thurman had also had the opportunity to meet Gandhi in 1936, and the dean told Martin about his conversations with the great leader.

Whenever Martin needed a break from his doctoral studies, he went to the William E. Carter Playground to play basketball. Martin also enjoyed spending time with his new friends and was often invited to dinner parties at their homes. In a town with so many new faces and interesting people to meet, it should be no surprise that Martin dated and was known as quite the ladies' man. But all that changed the day he met Coretta Scott.

LOVE AND MARRIAGE

Among Martin's many friends was a young woman named Mary Powell. Having both grown up in Atlanta, Martin and Mary were very close, and he trusted her judgment. By January 1952, Martin had grown tired of the dating scene and asked Mary if she knew any nice women he could date. It just so happened that Mary did have someone in mind—her friend and classmate Coretta Scott.

A student at New England Conservatory, Coretta was a talented violinist and singer. She was also beautiful and very kind. Mary was certain the two would make a great couple, and she gave Coretta's phone number to Martin.

Coretta didn't have to wait long. Martin called right away, and Coretta agreed to go out to lunch with him.

Martin was one of the fortunate students who had a car, a green Chevy. On their first date, he picked up Coretta and headed downtown to Sharaf's Cafeteria, a popular diner located on Massachusetts Avenue.

Although Martin was immediately taken by Coretta's beauty, her first impressions of him were very different. She thought Martin was too short and would have been more attractive with a mustache. But her opinion soon changed; over the course of the date, Coretta realized that Martin was a man of great substance.

Over lunch, the two discovered they had a lot in common and spent more time talking than eating. In addition to their shared love of music, Martin and Coretta had had similar childhoods. They were both from the South. Coretta was from a little city in Alabama called Marion. And because they'd both grown up under the laws of segregation, they knew what it was like to experience racism.

Much like Martin, Coretta was also very passionate

about equal rights. One of their first conversations was about racial injustice. By the end of their first date, Martin was love-struck.

On the drive home, Martin confessed, "You know, you have everything I ever wanted in a wife: intelligence, character, beauty, and personality. When can I see you again?"

After telling Mary all about their wonderful date, Martin felt forever indebted to his friend for playing matchmaker. "Mary, I owe you a thousand dollars for introducing me to this girl," he said excitedly.

Martin and Coretta continued to spend as much time as possible with each other. Coretta was smitten with Martin's intelligence and charisma. After dating for a few months, it came as no surprise that they were ready to meet each other's families. Coretta met Martin's parents when she visited him over the summer in Atlanta, and she saw them again a few months later when they visited Martin in Boston. Soon Coretta was calling Martin's parents "Daddy King" and "Mama King."

Even though they hadn't been dating for long, Martin knew he wanted to marry Coretta.

In April 1953, Martin and Coretta's engagement

was announced in the *Atlanta Daily World,* the city's only black newspaper.

On June 18, 1953, a little over a year after Mary introduced them, Coretta and Martin were married in Marion, Alabama. Reverend Martin Luther King Sr. officiated their wedding, which took place on the lawn of Coretta's childhood home.

CHAPTER 3

BOYCOTTING SEGREGATION

By 1954, Martin and Coretta were settled into their new married life, and Martin was finishing his studies at Boston University. As always, Martin remained focused on politics, and like most other Americans, he was eagerly awaiting the Supreme Court's decision in *Brown v. Board of Education*. The case had originated in Topeka, Kansas, where, like in the South, public schools were segregated by race. A black man named Oliver Brown had challenged the law as unconstitutional because it required his young daughter to ride a segregated bus to a blacks-only school that was much farther away than the whites-only school in their community. Twelve other black families with similar complaints had joined the lawsuit, and everyone was waiting to learn the fate of segregation in public schools.

On May 17, 1954, the Supreme Court issued its decision.

ENDED BY COURT

May 17, 1954

COURT BANS SEGREGATION IN PUBLIC SCHOOLS

May 17, 1954

SCHOOL SEGREGATION BANNED

May 17, 1954

SEGREGATION HELD TO BE UNCONSTITUTIONAL

Although this was a legal victory, the desegregation of public schools would be anything but a success story. There was outcry from white citizens in the South, who pleaded with lawmakers to reverse the decision. And in some states, like Virginia, rather than desegregate the schools, the government closed them altogether.

Of course, Martin considered the ruling a victory. Having had the opportunity to attend racially integrated universities, Martin knew the benefits of people of different races and nationalities learning from each other. He was excited that America had taken a major step toward equality, but it was just the beginning of a long battle. The civil rights movement was starting to brew.

THE MOVE TO MONTGOMERY

Before Martin finished his studies at Boston University, he was offered an exciting job. The pastoral board at Dexter Avenue Baptist Church had heard great things about him, and they were in need of a new pastor. There was only one problem—Dexter Avenue Baptist Church was located in Montgomery, Alabama.

Martin wanted to lead a ministry, and a well-respected church like Dexter Avenue Baptist Church would be a good opportunity to do so. Coretta had hopes of becoming a professional musician, and there were more opportunities for black women in the North. But ultimately she wanted to support Martin's dreams, and he believed that Montgomery was where God was calling him. He'd studied to become a preacher with the goal of helping the black community, and now it was time to begin. Coretta agreed to the move, and she told Martin that fighting for equality would be not just his work—it would become their work.

Martin began his job at Dexter Avenue Baptist Church on September 1, 1954. He also continued his theology studies, and in June 1955, Martin earned his doctoral degree in systematic theology from Boston University, which afforded him the title Dr. Martin Luther King Jr.

The congregation loved Martin's dynamic preaching style as well as his outspokenness on racial inequality. He challenged his church members and other black people in Montgomery not to wait for change but rather to be a part of the movement.

One of the first things Martin encouraged black people to do was register to vote. Even though black people had the right to vote, they often faced voter suppression when trying to register and at the polls. Martin knew that voting would be crucial in bringing about change—it would allow black people to elect officials who would fight for their rights.

Voter Suppression

Voter suppression is a method used to make it difficult for certain groups of people to vote in elections, or to stop them from voting altogether. Common examples include:

→ Requiring people to pay a poll tax in order to be eligible to vote. (Often these fees were very expensive or had to be paid in advance, which made it difficult for poor people to vote.)

→ Requiring voters to take literacy tests, which unfairly disadvantages people who are unable to read and write.

→ Closing polling stations in areas where a specific group of people lives.

Many of these requirements were enforced under Jim Crow laws. Prior to the Voting Rights Act of 1965, voter suppression frequently targeted racial minorities and women.

Martin also encouraged his church members to join the National Association for the Advancement of Colored People, also known as the NAACP. The organization supported the fight for equal political and civil rights for black people, and Martin knew there might come a time when the citizens of Montgomery would need the NAACP's help.

The NAACP

In 1908, race riots in Springfield, Illinois, resulted in the deaths of two black citizens as well as the burning and destruction of over 40 black businesses and homes. Leading black and white activists established the National Association for the Advancement of Colored People in February 1909 to address the racial violence happening across America. The NAACP's founding members included many well-known black activists, such as W. E. B. DuBois, Ida B. Wells-Barnett, and Mary Church Terrell. Lawyers who worked for the NAACP served as legal advocates for black people who believed they had been discriminated against, and the organization also helped labor unions demand equal wages for black workers. The NAACP quickly became known as a civil rights organization focused on ending racial violence and supporting racial and economic equality.

Black people across Montgomery began to notice that the new preacher in town was fighting to bring about change. And soon Martin's ministry and commitment to nonviolent activism would be put to the test.

A YEAR THAT SPARKED CHANGE

Even though *Brown v. Board of Education* had ruled to end segregation in public schools, many states remained resistant to desegregating their schools. In Alabama, the state invented new laws such as the pupil placement law of 1955, which allowed school boards, not parents, to determine where students would attend school. This was a cleverly disguised law to keep schools segregated. There was also an increase in new private schools, where it was still legal for classrooms to be whites-only. Some laws even gave school boards the right to close any school faced with desegregation.

As more black people challenged these segregation

laws, white citizens who wanted things to remain separate became increasingly violent. The year 1955 sparked change in the civil rights movement.

One of the first incidents occurred on March 2, 1955, when a teenager named Claudette Colvin was riding a Montgomery city bus home from school. When a white woman boarded the bus, the driver told Claudette to give up her seat. She refused.

Hoping to calm the situation, three other black passengers offered their seats to the white woman. But the white passenger wanted Claudette's seat—the only one where she wouldn't have to sit next to any black passengers. Even when the bus driver threatened and kicked Claudette, she remained seated.

Someone called the police, and Claudette was arrested and handcuffed. She was only fifteen years old. Worried and afraid, Claudette sat in a jail cell for several hours until her pastor paid her bail so she could go home.

Martin was concerned about Claudette's arrest for many reasons, including the fact that she'd boarded the bus on Highland Avenue—directly across from his church on Dexter Avenue.

The second incident that shocked the nation happened several months later, in August 1955, when fourteen-year-old Emmett Till of Chicago, Illinois, was spending time with his family in Mississippi. Emmett's mother knew that things were much more dangerous for black people in the South, and she had warned her son to be careful.

Like most boys his age, Emmett loved joking around. On August 24, 1955, Emmett was standing with his cousins and a few friends in front of a local store, Bryant's Grocery. One of Emmett's cousins, Curtis Jones, recalls Emmett showing them a picture of his classmates. Emmett pointed to a white girl in the photo, claiming she was his girlfriend. Of course, the boys didn't believe Emmett and issued a dare—to ask the white woman who was sitting at the store's counter for a date.

Emmett accepted the challenge and went into the store as the boys waited outside, watching through the window. No one knows for sure what Emmett said.

Laughing, the boys went about their day and thought nothing else of the matter. But when the store's owner, Roy Bryant, returned from a trip a few days later, his wife, Carolyn, told him what had happened. She had been the woman sitting at the counter. Carolyn said that Emmett had grabbed her and said inappropriate things, which wasn't true. Roy was furious, and on August 28, along with his half brother, J. W. Milam, he set out to find Emmett to make him pay for what he'd done.

Emmett was staying with his uncle Moses Wright, and when the two white men arrived at his house, Moses begged them to forgive his nephew. Emmett was just a young boy who was visiting from up North. He'd been playing around with his cousins and hadn't known to not speak to a white woman. But Roy and J. W. didn't care.

The two men forced Emmett into their car. A few days later, Emmett's body was found in the Tallahatchie River. He had been beaten so badly, his face was barely recognizable, and he'd also been shot in the head.

At Emmett's funeral, his mother demanded that his casket be open so the world could see what the killers had done to her son. She allowed reporters to take pictures and publish the photos of Emmett's beaten, swollen body. His senseless death was mourned throughout America, and approximately fifty thousand people went to personally view Emmett's body and pay their respects at Roberts Temple Church of God in Christ, in Chicago. The murder of a fourteen-year-old black boy simply because he'd spoken to a white woman showed just how bad life was in the racially segregated South. Despite testimony from Moses Wright, who identified Roy and J. W. as the men who took Emmett from his home, the two men were found not guilty of murder by an all-white jury, further enraging the nation.

What Happened to Carolyn Bryant?

Carolyn testified in court about what had occurred between her and Emmett Till. For over 60 years, she remained firm on her story. Then, in 2017, Carolyn publicly declared that she'd lied about Emmett grabbing her and making inappropriate comments. But nothing could be done to reopen the case and convict his killers. If Emmett had not been murdered, he would have been in his seventies when Carolyn confessed.

Amid the sadness following Emmett's murder, Coretta and Martin received a blessing. On November 17, 1955, Coretta gave birth to their first child, a daughter named Yolanda Denise. Her birth made Martin even more impassioned about racial equality. He wanted Yolanda and all black children to have the same opportunities as white children.

⋛ NOT GIVING IN ⋚

The events of 1955 came to a head on December 1, 1955, when a black passenger named Rosa Parks refused to give in to the unfair demands of segregation.

Along her bus route, as white passengers got onto the bus, the designated white section quickly filled. In order to make more room for the white passengers, the driver moved the sign that noted where black passengers could sit. He told the four black passengers in that section to stand up. Three of them complied, but Rosa did not get up. Outraged, the driver called the police and Rosa was arrested.

Black protesters gathered in front of the jail and demanded that Rosa be released. She was an important figure in the Montgomery chapter of the NAACP, and her arrest was the final straw. Black people were determined and willing to do whatever it took to end segregation. And they wanted Martin to help them.

Like much of Montgomery, Martin was angry about young Claudette's arrest, heartbroken over Emmett's horrific murder, and enraged by the treatment of Rosa.

In the days following Rosa's arrest, the black community in Montgomery discussed what could be done. E. D. Nixon, a civil rights activist, was among them. He'd previously served in a leadership role in the Montgomery NAACP. E. D. saw Rosa's arrest as an opportunity.

"When Rosa Parks was arrested, I thought 'this is it!' 'Cause she's morally clean, she's reliable, nobody had nothing on her, she had the courage of her convictions." —E. D. Nixon

He reached out to Jo Ann Robinson of the Women's Political Council for assistance, and together the group organized a boycott of Montgomery buses for one day. On the morning of December 5, almost the entire black community would refuse to use the buses, in protest. Seeing how much support they had, the organizers met later that afternoon to discuss how they could continue the boycott.

By the end of the meeting, the group had formed the Montgomery Improvement Association (MIA). Although they wanted to continue the bus boycott, their overall mission was to advance the status of Montgomery's black residents and improve race relations. Thanks to his growing reputation in Montgomery, Martin was elected to serve as the organization's chairman and president.

A PEACEFUL PROTEST

On December 6, 1955, the protest continued. Rather than ride Montgomery's segregated city buses, black people chose to walk, ride their bikes, or carpool. It was the first time black people had united in protest to bring about change in Montgomery, and they hoped their efforts would work.

In the following weeks, the MIA met with city officials to negotiate. They gave a list of their demands. White bus operators were often rude to black passengers, so the MIA wanted black people to be treated fairly. And on routes that had mostly black passengers, they wanted black drivers. They also asked that seating be on a first-come, first-served basis—no more requirements for black passengers to give up their seats or sit at the back of the bus. But city officials refused, and so the boycott continued.

At first, nothing happened. But as the weeks passed, and then months, city officials realized that the boycott was causing them to lose a lot of money. Black citizens made up a large percentage of Montgomery's population, and most had relied on public transportation. On some routes, the buses were completely empty. The more money that was lost, the angrier the city officials became. Soon city officials and white citizens who wanted the buses to remain segregated began to harass the peaceful protesters.

A PEACEFUL PROTEST TURNS VIOLENT

Some white citizens walked alongside the protesters, calling them names and even spitting on them. Police officers arrested the boycotters and forced them to pay costly fines. But Martin had known this might happen. It was one of the reasons why he'd wanted black people in Montgomery to become members of the NAACP—so they could ask the organization for help if they found themselves in trouble with the law.

The NAACP became one of the biggest supporters of the Montgomery bus boycott, providing legal aid to black protesters and raising money for those who had to pay fines.

In response, people who were against the boycott focused their anger on the leader of the boycott—Martin. But he remained firm in the face of threats: the Montgomery bus boycott would end only when city buses were desegregated and the MIA demands were met.

From sending angry letters in the mail to making threatening phone calls late at night, white people tried to intimidate Martin and force him to end the boycott. And one of the threats almost proved deadly. On the night of January 30, 1956, Coretta was at home alone with Yolanda while Martin attended a meeting about the protest. Without warning, someone threw a bomb at their house. Thankfully, there was little damage, and Martin was especially grateful that Coretta and Yolanda were unharmed. These events prompted a spiritual revelation in Martin that filled him with the strength to persevere in his efforts to end segregation. When a crowd gathered around his home, Martin insisted that protesters remain peaceful and nonviolent.

GAYLE V. BROWDER

The Montgomery bus boycott lasted almost thirteen months. It ended on December 20, 1956, following a US Supreme Court ruling that Alabama's laws requiring blacks and whites to be separated on public transportation were unconstitutional. The case was originally brought by Claudette Colvin and five other black passengers who felt their treatment on the city buses had been unfair. Public buses in Montgomery would no longer be segregated—black passengers could sit wherever they wanted, and they no longer had to give up their seats. The Montgomery bus boycott is considered the event that gave the civil rights movement momentum. And because Martin had led the MIA and the boycott, it placed him front and center of the movement.

CHAPTER 4

A MOVEMENT BEGINS

Throughout 1956, dozens of other, similar bus boycotts were held in segregated states, inspired by the protests in Montgomery. Members of the MIA and several black leaders wanted to figure out the best way to keep the momentum going. The group decided to meet in Atlanta, Georgia, on January 10, 1957.

Among the black leaders was a man named Ralph David Abernathy. He and Martin had met years before, when Ralph had been a graduate student at Atlanta University. After hearing Martin preach a sermon at Ebenezer Baptist Church, Ralph had introduced himself, and the two men had quickly become close friends. They had a lot in common. Both were Baptist ministers with a passion for civil rights.

The Role of the Black Church

Since the time when the first Africans arrived in America and were baptized, religion has played an important role in black people's lives. They sang spirituals to help them endure slavery, and later to pass messages to help them escape. The church was seen as a haven—a place for black people to worship and to celebrate, and in troubled times to mourn together. During segregation, there were few places where black people could meet to discuss issues affecting their community—except for at church. Like Martin Luther King Jr., many other black pastors were influential leaders in their communities.

At the January meeting in Atlanta, the leaders founded the Southern Christian Leadership Conference (SCLC) and stated their vision: civil rights are essential to democracy, segregation must end, and all black people should reject segregation absolutely and nonviolently. Martin was elected president and Ralph was chosen as the financial secretary-treasurer. The SCLC would become one of the most important organizations in the civil rights movement.

The SCLC

Founded in 1957, the Southern Christian Leadership Conference made nonviolent mass protests the cornerstone of their strategy in the civil rights movement. Unlike many other civil rights organizations at that time, SCLC membership was open to everyone, regardless of race, religion, or background.

⋛ DEMANDING EQUALITY ⋛

After the success of the Montgomery bus boycott and with the support of organizations like the NAACP and the newly formed SCLC, black people felt more empowered to demand equality beyond public transportation. Throughout the nation, they began to protest for fair housing, employment opportunities, and voting rights. They wanted equal rights and fair treatment in every aspect of their lives.

One of the most noted acts of black people enforcing integration occurred on September 4, 1957, in Little Rock, Arkansas. It was the first day of classes at Little Rock Central High School. And it was the first day that the formerly all-white school would have black students. Nine black students enrolled, but some white families didn't want them there. Arkansas governor Orval Faubus called the National Guard to block the school's entrance so that the black students couldn't go inside.

But not everyone in Little Rock agreed with the governor's decision. The Little Rock School District issued a statement condemning the use of soldiers and asked citizens to participate in a citywide prayer service. And the mayor of Little Rock asked President

Dwight D. Eisenhower to help. The president issued an order that required the National Guard to protect the nine black students when they went to school.

The Little Rock Nine

The nine black students who integrated Little Rock Central High School were Minnijean Brown, Elizabeth Eckford, Ernest Green, Thelma Mothershed, Melba Pattillo, Gloria Ray, Terrence Roberts, Jefferson Thomas, and Carlotta Walls. With the support of their parents and the Arkansas NAACP, each student received counseling to help them prepare for starting at the mainly white school. Despite the dangers, the Little Rock Nine persisted and are nationally recognized for the important roles they played in the civil rights movement. As adults, they each received a prestigious Congressional Gold Medal in 1999, and America's first black president, Barack Obama, personally invited them to his inauguration in 2009.

⋛ FAME AND DANGER ⋚

Martin was now also in the spotlight. On December 21, 1956, people around the nation celebrated when Martin was one of the first citizens to ride Montgomery's desegregated buses. The victory of the nonviolent protest made Martin famous. And on May 17, 1957, he gave his first national address at the Prayer Pilgrimage for Freedom in Washington, DC, where twenty thousand people gathered in support to listen to speeches and to hear songs performed by famous gospel singers like Mahalia Jackson. Martin ended the event with a celebrated speech, "Give Us the Ballot," that urged the president and Congress to help black people in their fight for civil rights.

President Eisenhower had the challenge of enforcing the Supreme Court's ruling to desegregate public schools, and Martin wrote to him several times, inviting him to meet with black civil rights leaders. He finally agreed to meet with Martin on June 23, 1958.

Prior to the meeting, the civil rights leaders drafted a statement to the president that offered ideas to help deal with desegregation and racism, including a White House conference on race relations. The meeting lasted for forty-five minutes, and although President Eisenhower promised to consider the black leaders' recommendations, he did not promise to take further action. After the meeting, Martin shared his thoughts with reporters:

> There is a desperate need for channels of communication to be opened between Negro and white citizens particularly in the South.

Martin spent much of the remaining summer finishing his first book, and on September 17, 1958, *Stride Toward Freedom: The Montgomery Story* was published. Martin was proud of the book and felt it was more than his story alone.

"[*Stride Toward Freedom*] is the chronicle of 50,000 Negroes who took to heart the principles of nonviolence, who learned to fight for their rights with the weapon of love, and who, in the process, acquired a new estimate of their own human worth."
—Martin Luther King Jr.

But not everyone was excited about Martin's success. At a book signing in Harlem, New York, a woman named Izola Ware Curry stabbed Martin in the chest with a seven-inch letter opener. He almost died. Thankfully, Martin was rushed to Harlem Hospital, where doctors managed to save his life. According to medical records, the letter opener's blade was so close to a main artery in Martin's heart that if he had so much as sneezed, the stabbing would have been fatal.

THE KINGS VISIT INDIA

Martin's brush with death made him more focused on the things he wanted to achieve in his lifetime. Martin continued to study Gandhi's teachings and mention him in his speeches. Martin had had quite a few opportunities to visit the homeland of the man who'd served as an inspiration, but there'd always been a conflict. But after surviving being stabbed, Martin wouldn't put off his trip to India any longer.

Martin asked his wife and a family friend who also worked with the MIA, Lawrence Reddick, to join him. On February 3, 1959, Lawrence and the Kings departed from New York for a five-week trip.

The Kings were treated like royalty in India. As people of color who had been mistreated by Europeans under British rule, India's citizens could relate to black people's struggles. And, of course, they valued Martin for his admiration and respect for Gandhi.

Martin received so many invitations, it was impossible to go to every event. Still, the events the Kings did attend, and the people they met, had a profound impact on their lives. They discovered that the people of India loved listening to African American spirituals, and as an accomplished singer, Coretta was honored to perform at public events. One of the highlights of the Kings' visit was when they met some of Gandhi's friends and supporters. It was a very meaningful experience for Martin, and spending time in Gandhi's home brought him even closer to the man he admired so much.

> Since being in India, I am more convinced than ever before that the method of nonviolent resistance is the most potent weapon available to oppressed people.

After the Kings' trip to India, the family moved to Atlanta so that Martin could work more closely with the SCLC, which was based there. Martin had a very busy schedule, and living near the organization's headquarters would make life much easier. And there was another bonus—Martin joined his father as assistant pastor of Ebenezer Baptist Church.

STUDENTS JOIN THE MOVEMENT

The Montgomery bus boycott not only inspired adults across the nation; it also inspired young people. On February 1, 1960, the first student-led nonviolent protest began in North Carolina. Ezell Blair Jr., David Richmond, Franklin McCain, and Joseph McNeil were students at the Agricultural and Technical College of North Carolina, a historically black college in

Greensboro. Like many other young people at the time, they had been deeply moved by Emmett Till's death five years before. They'd been around the same age as Emmett when he was murdered. Now they felt they were old enough to take action.

To protest segregated restaurants, the four black men went to Woolworth's, a popular store, and quietly sat at the lunch counter. Woolworth's had a policy of only serving white people at the lunch counter.

Store employees asked the four students to move, and then asked them to leave, but the men remained seated. Frustrated, store employees called the police. But the men weren't breaking any laws—they were just sitting quietly. The four men stayed seated until the store closed, and the next morning when Woolworth's opened for business, more students joined the sit-in.

By February 5, less than a week later, more than three hundred local students had joined the protest at Woolworth's. And because they were taking space from paying customers as well as causing a scene, Woolworth's and surrounding businesses lost money. Television coverage of the Greensboro sit-in inspired other college students, and soon white and black college students throughout the nation were holding sit-ins to protest segregation policies in other public places like libraries and beaches.

Black students who participated in sit-ins were denied service or told that the place where they were sitting was "whites-only." In restaurants, white patrons often poured milk and juice on students' heads or dumped food on them while laughing or taunting. But as long as the students sat still and remained quiet, they could only be arrested for minor offenses like disturbing the peace or disorderly conduct. The NAACP helped pay fines associated with the sit-ins.

Throughout 1960 and 1961, approximately seventy thousand black and white protesters participated in sit-ins that resulted in the integration of public facilities. One of the biggest success stories happened right where it all began—at Woolworth's in Greensboro. In late July 1960, the store integrated its lunch counter, and the first black people to eat there were Woolworth's employees Geneva Tisdale, Susie Morrison, Anetha Jones, and Charles Best.

Student Nonviolent Coordinating Committee (SNCC)

With the help of civil rights organizer and SCLC official Ella Baker, more than 200 students founded the Student Nonviolent Coordinating Committee (SNCC) in April 1960. Many student activists had grown up attending civil rights meetings with their parents, and almost every chapter of the NAACP had a Youth Council. In 1961, SNCC students participated in Freedom Rides. They rode public buses from the North into the South to test a recent US Supreme

Court ruling that made segregation on interstate transportation unconstitutional. As buses entered Southern states, Freedom Riders were often met with violence from white protesters and were arrested by police.

The civil rights movement was now at the forefront of American politics, and Martin was concerned about how dangerous it was becoming. He worried about the safety of Coretta and Yolanda, as well as his son, Martin Luther King III, who'd been born in 1957.

Martin was also anxious about his own well-being. State and local governments were always finding ways to charge him for crimes that could land him in prison. On February 17, 1960, the state of Alabama claimed he'd lied on income tax returns. Martin was the only person ever to be tried for this crime in Alabama. Everyone knew he was being targeted because of his involvement in the civil rights movement. Ultimately a jury of twelve white men found Martin not guilty. The verdict gave Martin hope, but the fight was far from over, and Martin's commitment to nonviolent protests would be challenged many more times.

CHAPTER 5

THE FIGHT FOR CIVIL RIGHTS

The late 1950s and early 1960s were crucial years in America's struggle for equality, and Martin was considered a key figure. In addition to giving sermons and speaking on behalf of SCLC, Martin gave interviews to newspaper and television reporters. In 1957, Martin gained national attention when *Time* magazine featured him on its cover. In that same issue, *Time* published an article on Martin's work with the Montgomery bus boycott and named the young pastor "one of the nation's remarkable leaders."

"Across the South . . . Negro leaders look toward Montgomery, Ala., the cradle of the Confederacy, for advice and counsel."
—*Time*

Early in the civil rights movement, black people made up the majority of Martin's supporters, but by the 1960s, Martin had won over the hearts and minds of many white people as well. Although this was a great success for the movement, those who were against equal rights for black people saw this as problematic. It was not uncommon for Martin to receive hate letters in the mail or threatening phone calls in which people vowed to kill him and his family. Sometimes Martin was even harassed by the police in a city he was visiting.

Police Brutality

For several decades following the abolition of slavery, only white men were allowed to serve on the police force. Many police officers were former Confederate soldiers and members of hate groups that discriminated against black people. They often abused their power by threatening, intimidating, and even killing black people. This violence continued throughout the civil rights movement even in the midst of peaceful protests. In modern America, there continue to be reasons for black communities to distrust some police officers, and organizations such as Black Lives Matter have formed to seek justice.

On October 19, 1960, Martin was among over fifty protesters who took part in a department store sit-in. Located in Atlanta, Rich's department store had a special restaurant and fitting room area called the Magnolia Room. Even though black people could purchase items from Rich's, only white people could sit in the Magnolia Room and try on clothes there. When Martin and the other protesters entered the Magnolia Room and refused to leave, the police arrested them. Eventually everyone was released—except Martin.

The police decided to detain Martin for a previous offense. They gave him a four-month sentence and transferred him to the state prison in Reidsville, Georgia, where he would be required to do hard labor. But thankfully, Martin had the support of a very influential white political family—the Kennedys.

Senator John F. Kennedy was one of the nation's presidential hopefuls, and he'd met with Martin just a few weeks before his arrest. The two men had discussed black people's fight for equality, and Martin had encouraged the young senator to show his support for the cause. Then, when Martin was in prison, he sought help from Kennedy. The senator was not only sympathetic to Martin's plea, but with the presidential election less than a month away, he needed the black community's votes. Kennedy's younger brother Robert was also active in politics. In fact, he left his job to help his older brother with his presidential campaign. Together, the brothers convinced a judge to grant Martin bond. Martin was relieved and extremely grateful when he was released from the Reidsville prison on October 27.

A Historic Phone Call

In the early-morning hours on Wednesday, October 26, 1960, one telephone call helped change the course of history. Senator John F. Kennedy knew that this call would lose him votes in the white community, and quite possibly the election altogether. Still, he made a call to ask the unthinkable—he wanted Georgia's governor, Ernest Vandiver, to have Martin released from the Reidsville state prison. Senator Kennedy faced severe backlash when Martin was released the next day, but Kennedy would go on to win the presidential election on November 8, 1960.

After his release, Martin continued to travel across the country. He toured around Georgia and visited many cities in Alabama, too, including Montgomery, Birmingham, and Selma. He also went to the Carolinas and to Memphis, Tennessee.

Whenever it was possible, Martin attended nonviolent protests taking place in these cities, walking side by side and arm in arm with his supporters.

THE ALBANY MOVEMENT

Unfortunately, not all of Martin's protests were successful. In 1961, Martin traveled to Albany, Georgia, with the SNCC, SCLC, and NAACP to protest segregation policies. Before the protest, the police set up roadblocks to make it difficult for people to march. When arrested, Martin chose to go to jail rather than pay a fine, in the hope that his imprisonment would bring attention to the movement. But city officials were now more prepared to deal with protesters and to make sure they didn't receive a lot of press coverage. And so the police let Martin go after only three days, knowing that if he were imprisoned for much longer, it would attract national attention.

Although there were a few small changes in Albany's segregation policies, after almost a year, the Albany protests ended without much success.

≳ THE SUMMER OF 1962 ≲

In late July 1962, Martin attended a prayer vigil in Albany. It was intended as a day of atonement following several incidents of racial violence in the city. And yet, ironically, Martin was again arrested at the peaceful event.

Charged with disturbing the peace, obstructing the path of a sidewalk, and protesting without a permit, Martin spent another two weeks in jail before an anonymous person paid for his release in early August.

Then, barely one month later, Martin was attacked by a member of a hate group during an SCLC conference in Birmingham, Alabama. The SCLC meeting was open to everyone, regardless of race, and a white man named Roy James saw this as a good opportunity to get close to Martin. And Roy wasn't just another angry white citizen; he was a member of a very powerful hate group—the American Nazi Party.

American Nazi Party

The American Nazi Party is one of America's oldest and largest hate groups. In addition to discriminating against Jews, racial minorities, and members of the LGBTQ+ community, the white people who become members idolize Adolf Hitler and believe that anyone not of white European ancestry is inferior to them.

During Martin's speech, Roy rushed to the stage. At six feet two, he was significantly taller and stronger than Martin, who was five feet seven. Roy punched Martin so hard on his left cheek that Martin staggered backward. The audience screamed and gasped in disbelief as Roy continued to punch Martin. After catching his footing, Martin turned to Roy, and rather than fight back, he dropped his hands to his sides, refusing to fight violence with violence.

Later the two men went to a private room, where they spoke to each other calmly without any further violence. Martin didn't want to press charges for the assault, but the police still arrested Roy. He was ordered to serve thirty days in jail and pay a twenty-five-dollar fine. Thankfully, the attack hadn't turned deadly. Still, it reflected just how unsettling and dangerous the civil rights movement had become.

BIRMINGHAM CAMPAIGN

Alabama had always been a dangerous state for black protesters, but by 1963, things were even worse under the leadership of the state's new governor, George Wallace. In addition to opposing integration, Governor Wallace openly supported the Ku Klux Klan (KKK). Protesters knew that no matter how peaceful their approach, they would be met with violence by citizens and law officials.

Nevertheless, Martin helped organize peaceful demonstrations to protest several of the stores and businesses that refused to hire black people in Birmingham. Even though many other Southern cities had already desegregated public places, things were so bad in Birmingham that some of their public restrooms remained segregated!

Eugene "Bull" Connor, Birmingham's commissioner of public safety, oversaw the city's law enforcement, and he was determined to make things as difficult as possible for Martin. Like the governor, Commissioner Connor openly supported the KKK and made it widely known that he was in favor of segregation.

When the Birmingham campaign began in early April 1963, Commissioner Connor showed just how determined he was to keep Birmingham racially divided.

The first demonstrations took place on April 3 as protesters staged sit-ins at local lunch counters. More sit-ins and marches took place over the next several days, and protesters were arrested. On April 7, Commissioner Connor ordered his department to use police dogs to help disperse the crowds.

But protesters continued to demonstrate until April 11, when civil rights leaders received an important legal document. It was an order from the local court that stated the leaders were not allowed to boycott, hold sit-ins, or participate in similar types of protest behavior in Birmingham. If they didn't comply, they would be arrested.

Martin knew there would be serious consequences if he defied the order. He would likely have to serve time in jail again. However, in the same way that the police had learned the best strategies for dealing with protesters, those who were on the front lines of the movement had learned the best ways to deal with police. If Martin or any of the other protesters were arrested, they planned to use their imprisonment to bring attention to the racist practices in Birmingham. In fact, Martin hoped that so many protesters would be arrested that they would overcrowd the jail.

Determined to continue the Birmingham campaign, civil rights leaders chose to defy the court order the very next day. And on April 12, Martin was among those who were arrested. As he sat in his jail cell, he was so angered and shocked by the violence in Birmingham that he felt compelled to write about his experience. In a powerful piece of writing that would become known as "Letter from Birmingham Jail," Martin spoke of the horrors of segregation and shared how much racism hurt the black community. Martin's words were so powerful that the letter was shared on national television. It would become one of his most famous writings.

It is unfortunate that demonstrations are taking place in Birmingham, but it is even more unfortunate that the city's white power structure left the Negro community with no alternative.

Nonviolent marches and sit-ins continued throughout April, and there were many more arrests. Still, supporters of the Birmingham campaign showed no signs of giving up. And in early May, a surprising number of new supporters joined in the fight for equality in Birmingham—children.

On May 2, 1963, over a thousand members of the black community showed up to support the Birmingham protest, including children as young as eight years old. They were part of the Children's Crusade, a group of young people who participated in nonviolent protests with their parents' permission. Those following news coverage of the Birmingham campaign watched in horror as hundreds of children and teenagers were arrested. But soon, participants in the Children's Crusade would face even more violence.

Commissioner Connor told Birmingham police to prepare for more protesters the next day. And this time, the officers weren't alone—their police dogs were with them. As the crowd of children and teenage protesters moved forward, the police and their dogs were given orders to attack.

Camera footage captured the police beating protesters with batons. The growling dogs bared their teeth and bit people as they tried to run away. Commissioner Connor also ordered the fire department to use high-pressure hoses to spray the crowd. The water was so powerful that it knocked many protesters off their feet.

Protesters had never encountered such violence from police before, and it was especially upsetting to see children being treated so inhumanely. In the end, those who were unable to escape were arrested.

Due to the media attention surrounding Martin's "Letter from Birmingham Jail" and the Children's Crusade, the Birmingham campaign was ultimately successful. After the protest, many of Birmingham's segregation laws were abolished.

CHAPTER 6

THE MARCH ON WASHINGTON

Martin now had the support of lawmakers in Washington. When John F. Kennedy had helped Martin get released from prison in 1960, Martin had publicly thanked the senator, and many black voters took note of Kennedy's support. They returned the favor the following month, when at the November 1960 election they gave Kennedy their vote for president. Democrat Kennedy defeated Republican Richard Nixon by less than 1 percent in the popular vote, and the narrow victory highlighted the importance of the role black voters had played.

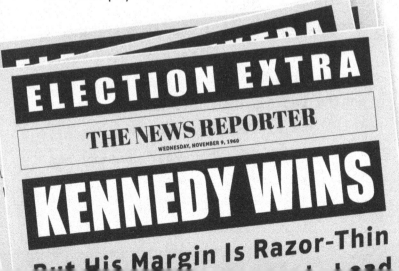

President John F. Kennedy

President John F. Kennedy, commonly referred to by his nickname JFK, was born on May 29, 1917, in Brookline, Massachusetts. He hailed from a family known for politics, so it was no surprise when JFK was elected as a US senator from Massachusetts in 1952. Beloved and admired by his constituents, Senator Kennedy became America's 35th president eight years later. During his term, President Kennedy founded the internationally recognized Peace Corps, a volunteer organization that sends American students overseas to help developing countries. He was also known for his work during the civil rights movement, including meeting with Martin and other leaders with the hope of ending racial violence. Many people still use his words for encouragement, such as "Ask not what your country can do for you—ask what you can do for your country."

A few years into his presidency, Kennedy tried to introduce a civil rights law. But too many people in Congress still agreed with segregation, and the bill did not receive enough votes. On June 11, 1963, Kennedy gave a powerful speech, broadcast over the radio and on TV, addressing the nation regarding the horrible violence that had occurred in Birmingham. The speech presented civil rights as a moral cause that required the efforts of all citizens.

Reactions to the speech were mixed, with Southern legislators not happy at all. But Martin was pleased. He felt the president had spoken well on the issue and believed that it would make a difference.

And on June 19, President Kennedy followed up his speech with a new civil rights bill he hoped would put an end to segregation in schools, restaurants, hotels, and other public places. Martin and his fellow activists felt that the best way to support the bill would be to organize a mass demonstration in the nation's capital—Washington, DC.

PLANNING THE MARCH

Civil rights leaders A. Philip Randolph and Bayard Rustin, spurred on by Kennedy's presidency and a need to focus on gaining economic equality, began organizing a march. As Martin and more civil rights groups got involved with the plan, they established the Council for United Civil Rights Leadership, which would coordinate funds and publicity for the event. Martin began working closely with James Farmer, John Lewis, A. Philip Randolph, Roy Wilkins, and Whitney Young Jr. This group of leaders became known as the Big Six.

The Big Six

1. **Martin Luther King Jr.**—Chairman of the SCLC

2. **James Farmer**—Founder of the Congress of Racial Equity (CORE)

3. **John Lewis**—Director of the SNCC

4. **A. Philip Randolph**—Organizer of one of the first black labor unions, the Brotherhood of Sleeping Car Porters

5. **Roy Wilkins**—Executive Secretary of the NAACP

6. **Whitney Young Jr.**—Executive Director of the National Urban League

A black woman named Dorothy Height was also involved in organizing the March on Washington. She served as president of the National Council of Negro Women. Despite not being included in the Big Six, Dorothy was instrumental in ensuring that the march focused on advancing opportunities for black women, their families, and their communities.

On June 22, 1963, the Big Six held a meeting with President Kennedy, who had concerns about the march. He feared the event would create "an atmosphere of intimidation" if hundreds of thousands of people descended on Washington. But Martin and his fellow activists insisted on following through with the march. They reassured Kennedy that it would be a peaceful march, not a violent protest. Kennedy eventually agreed and offered to help organize it.

As awareness of the march increased, more and more civil rights groups put their differences aside and came out to endorse the event. They combined their various goals and motivations to create a list of purposes for the march:

→ Pass civil rights legislation.

→ End school segregation.

→ Develop programs for the unemployed.

→ Make discrimination illegal.

→ Create a nationwide minimum wage.

→ Enforce the Fourteenth Amendment.

⋛ THE BIG TEN ⋚

On July 2, 1963, the Big Six met at the Roosevelt Hotel in New York to finalize plans. With the march less than eight weeks away, the men made a strategic decision—they invited four white leaders to join them. They wanted to encourage white citizens to attend the march and stand in solidarity with them.

The four white men who joined the Big Six were Reverend Eugene Carson Blake, president of the National Council of Churches; Walter Reuther, president of the United Automobile Workers; Mathew Ahmann, executive director of the National Catholic Conference for Interracial Justice; and Joachim Prinz, president of the American Jewish Congress. The Big Six plus these four men were often referred to as the Big Ten.

MARCHING FOR FREEDOM

Although there were challenges in the lead-up to the day, such as the expensive sound system being sabotaged (thankfully, it was repaired in time for the event!), on the morning of August 28, 1963, everything was in place for the protest. There were private marshals on hand, prepared to assist in case of violence, and they had strict orders not to harm protesters. There was also some concern that people might get too fired up during the speeches and cause the crowd to react. So, just in case, a government official had authority to cut off the sound system if things got rowdy. It seemed every precaution had been taken. The only thing left to do was wait to see how many people would gather at the Lincoln Memorial to attend the March on Washington.

The Significance of the Lincoln Memorial

Built in 1922, the large statute of President Abraham Lincoln overlooks the National Mall in the nation's capital. Dedicated with the hope of helping America heal from its division after the Civil War, the memorial is considered a symbol of freedom.

Over 250,000 black and white citizens heeded the call to campaign for equal rights and freedoms for all Americans. Although the crowd largely consisted of black attendees, between 75,000 and 95,000 white people joined them. Famous white musicians such as Bob Dylan sang alongside black gospel artists like Mahalia Jackson. It was the showing of solidarity that the Big Ten had hoped for, and more.

Before the March on Washington, the biggest protest in the US had occurred on August 8, 1925, when forty thousand KKK members marched in the nation's capital. Now, almost forty years later, protesters were gathering for a very different cause, and they were much larger in number. In fact, when members of the American Nazi Party tried to stage a counterprotest, it was obvious how insignificant they were in comparison to those supporting the march, and the small hate group quickly dispersed.

Local college students left their campuses to attend. Federal workers asked for permission to participate. And thousands of other citizens arrived by train, plane, and car to take part in the historic march.

Some attendees linked arms with strangers and sang African American spirituals as they gathered on the National Mall. There was excitement in the air as the peaceful crowd joined together in support of America's civil rights movement.

The program began with Marian Anderson leading the throng in singing the national anthem, followed by A. Philip Randolph's opening remarks. Later, journalist and activist Daisy Bates delivered a tribute to black women freedom fighters, and members of the Big Ten spoke about the need for equality and offered prayers for the nation. Speakers such as Rabbi Joachim Prinz spoke to the white people in attendance about the dangers of sitting back and watching injustice take place. As a German immigrant who had escaped the horrors of the Holocaust, Rabbi Prinz knew firsthand what happened when people failed to speak out against injustice done to their neighbors.

"America must not become a nation of onlookers. America must not remain silent." —Rabbi Joachim Prinz

Martin was the last leader to speak, and his speech would resonate with listeners all over the globe. It remains one of the most quoted speeches of all time.

After Martin's speech, A. Philip Randolph asked the crowd to take a pledge to commit to the struggle and support the fight against segregation and racism.

> I pledge my heart and my mind and my body unequivocally and without regard to personal sacrifice, to the achievement of social peace through social justice.

The crowd responded with a resounding, "I do pledge!"

The March on Washington concluded with one of Martin's first mentors, Morehouse College president Dr. Benjamin E. Mays, giving a blessing. Then, in a beautiful moment of solidarity, the crowd joined together to sing the anthem of the civil rights movement, "We Shall Overcome."

Given the success of the march, President Kennedy scheduled a meeting with the Big Ten and other march leaders immediately afterward. The group met him at the White House, and he congratulated them on the peaceful demonstration. As the march had been so well attended and successful, President Kennedy hoped it would improve the chances that Congress would support his civil rights act.

⋛ THE VIOLENCE CONTINUES ⋚

Although the march was considered a great success, many people in the South continued to oppose desegregation and equal rights for black people. And less than one month after the March on Washington, another tragedy occurred that rocked the nation to its core.

On Sunday, September 15, 1963, an act of racial violence devastated the civil rights movement. Shortly after the 10:00 a.m. service began at Birmingham's 16th Street Baptist Church, a bomb exploded, injuring twenty-two members of the mainly black church. It had been set by four members of the KKK. As more information emerged, people learned that the damage was even worse than they'd feared—four young black girls had been killed in the bombing. The victims were fourteen-year-olds Addie Mae Collins, Cynthia Wesley, and Carole Robertson and eleven-year-old Denise McNair. Thousands of angry black citizens gathered at the destroyed church to mourn the victims, and soon violence broke out across the city, resulting in the deaths of two young black men. Over eight thousand people attended the funerals for the girls on

September 18, where Martin delivered their eulogy.

Sadly, just a few months later, Martin was again devastated when President Kennedy was assassinated, on November 22, 1963.

> "In spite of the darkness of this hour, . . . we must not become bitter. . . . Life is hard, at times as hard as crucible steel. [But] today, you do not walk alone."
> —Martin Luther King Jr.

The Assassination of President Kennedy

On November 22, 1963, the nation mourned the assassination of President Kennedy. He was in Dallas, Texas, for a business trip, hoping to win the votes of Texans in the following year's election. The Texas governor, John Connally, suggested driving through the busy Dealey Plaza so the crowds could see the president and his wife, Jacqueline.

But in a building along the route, former US Marine Lee Harvey Oswald was waiting for his chance. As the Kennedys passed by, he fired three shots, one of which struck JFK in the neck, a wound that killed the president thirty minutes later. Oswald was arrested an hour afterward. He was shot and killed by Dallas club owner Jack Ruby on November 24, 1963, while being transferred from the city jail to the county jail.

John F. Kennedy's death was a great loss for the nation and the civil rights movement.

CHAPTER 7

A NEW AMERICA

Even though many unfair laws had been changed, there was still opposition to the new laws being enforced, and more work was needed to make Martin's dream of equality come true. Now, with more support than ever before, Martin was determined to help shape a new America. And finally, in 1964, Martin saw the success that he had worked so hard for.

THE CIVIL RIGHTS ACT OF 1964

In the aftermath of the events of 1963, including Kennedy's assassination and the Baptist church bombing, there was more support than ever for the civil rights bill. As a result, Kennedy's successor, President Lyndon B. Johnson, signed the Civil Rights Act of 1964 on July 2. President Johnson said that no speech or memorial could honor Kennedy's memory better than the passage of the bill that had meant so much to him.

It was a breakthrough law, granting every American equal civil rights and making it illegal to discriminate against someone based on their race, color, religion, sex, or national origin. The act also ensured fairer voter registration requirements and ended racial segregation in schools, businesses, and other public places.

Without Martin's tireless efforts and those of his supporters, the Civil Rights Act might never have been signed into law. But his nonstop schedule of attending meetings and giving speeches often left Martin exhausted. In early December 1964, Martin was admitted to St. Joseph's Infirmary in Atlanta for exhaustion. Doctors had ordered him to get some rest, so Martin was surprised when he received a phone call from Coretta.

Martin was shocked to learn that he'd been awarded the Nobel Peace Prize, one of the world's most distinguished awards. It was international recognition of his nonviolent approach to social justice, and Martin considered the prize a great honor and achievement.

The Nobel Peace Prize

Established in 1895 by famous Swedish inventor and manufacturer Alfred Nobel, the Nobel Peace Prize honors a person who has "done the most or the best work for fraternity between nations, the abolition or reduction of standing armies, and for the holding and promotion of peace congresses." Other notable Nobel Peace Prize award recipients include Holocaust survivor Elie Wiesel (1986); South African apartheid activist Nelson Mandela (1993); former president Barack Obama (2009); and Pakistani activist for female education Malala Yousafzai (2014), who was the youngest person to ever win the award. Mohandas Gandhi, Martin's role model, was nominated but never received the Nobel Peace Prize, so it was particularly special for Martin to win it.

When Martin accepted the prize on December 10, 1964, in Oslo, Norway, it wasn't just for himself. He accepted the award on behalf of everyone who had participated in the civil rights movement, and he donated the money he received to further advance equality. At the time, Martin was just thirty-five years old. And on that day, he was the youngest man and the second black person to ever receive the prestigious award.

⋝ THE STRUGGLE CONTINUES ⋜

The next phase of the civil rights movement would focus on enforcing the rights and freedoms granted under the Civil Rights Act, and Martin knew this would be as dangerous as the early years of the movement. State and local governments had operated under segregation and discriminatory laws for many years, and the Civil Rights Act would not make them immediately change their stance on equality. Rather, the passage of the new law would make some people even angrier and more resistant.

One area that still needed significant reform was voting. After years of violence, black people were afraid to register and cast their votes during elections. This was especially the case in the Deep South. Knowing how much power the president and Congress had, Martin met with President Johnson on February 9, 1965, to discuss voting rights. But little changed. In fact, one Sunday in 1965 was so violent, it became known as Bloody Sunday.

Bloody Sunday

Along with other activists in the SCLC and SNCC, Martin helped establish the Selma voting rights campaign in an effort to register more black voters in Alabama. The plan included a series of nonviolent marches, and more than 3,000 protesters were arrested between January 2 and February 7. Their efforts resulted in fewer than 100 new voters.

On February 18, a young black man named Jimmie Lee Jackson was among the protesters when police arrived. Jimmie fled the scene, but one of the police officers followed and shot him. His death sparked outrage throughout Alabama, and on March 7, about

600 protesters planned to march peacefully from Selma, Alabama, to the state capital, Montgomery, to commemorate Jimmie's senseless death. They also hoped to bring attention to voter suppression.

But they never made it to Montgomery. While attempting to cross the Edmund Pettus bridge, the protesters were doused with tear gas and beaten by law enforcement, forcing them to turn back. The brutal attack was captured by news cameras and broadcast across the nation, garnering even more support for the civil rights movement.

In response to the events of Bloody Sunday, Martin wanted to lead a symbolic march along the original planned route. In a surprise ruling, the federal district court judge, Frank M. Johnson Jr., ruled in favor of the demonstrators.

So on March 21, approximately 3,200 demonstrators left Selma and headed to Montgomery. But this time there was no violence, because the group was protected by hundreds of Alabama National Guardsmen. It was a grueling journey, but Martin led the protesters, boosting spirits by singing African American spirituals and gospel songs. During the day, the protesters walked up to twelve miles, and at night they slept in fields and watched out for one another. Along the way, something unexpected happened. As the protesters passed through small towns and cities, some of the residents joined them. When the group finally reached the steps of Alabama's capitol on Thursday, March 25, more than twenty thousand people had joined the march, and Martin proudly addressed those who had endured.

> "There never was a moment in American history more honorable and more inspiring than the pilgrimage of clergymen and laymen of every race and faith pouring into Selma to face danger at the side of its embattled Negroes."

The numbers showed just how unified and powerful black people in the South had become. And the campaign caught the attention of the president, who signed the Voting Rights Act of 1965 into law less than five months after the march, on August 6, 1965. It abolished voter suppression tactics and the many unfair requirements that had previously kept black people from exercising their right to vote.

THE DANGERS OF SEEKING EQUALITY

By the middle of the 1960s, Martin was all too familiar with the dangers of seeking equal civil rights for every American. Still, he took drastic steps to bring attention to the plight of the less fortunate when, in January 1966, he moved his family into a poor apartment complex in Chicago to protest housing discrimination. This bold move ultimately led to violence later that summer, when Martin became involved in the Chicago Freedom Movement.

On August 5, 1966, when Martin led a march near an all-white Chicago neighborhood, the group was attacked with bottles, rocks, and firecrackers.

Approximately thirty people were injured, including Martin, who was hit in the head with a brick. Still, the movement continued through to 1967. Many believe that Martin's work in Chicago inspired the Fair Housing Act, which was part of the Civil Rights Act of 1968.

In addition to its civil rights issues, America was dealing with military conflict in Vietnam. By 1967, thousands of US soldiers had been drafted and killed in the Vietnam War—a war that Martin openly opposed.

The Vietnam War

Conflict broke out between communist North Vietnam and anti-communist South Vietnam on November 1, 1955. America viewed Communism as a political threat to democracy. And so, on March 8, 1965, President Johnson ordered the first 3,500 US Marines to assist South Vietnam in combat.

At first, most Americans supported the decision, but as the number of injured soldiers and deaths increased, more citizens began to oppose the war. Young people were at the forefront of the anti-war movement because they were the ones being sent to fight in Vietnam. A military draft was in effect, requiring young men to register with the government. Men were selected according to a lottery system for mandatory enrollment in the armed forces. Approximately 80 percent of the men drafted to fight in the Vietnam War were lower-class, black, and Latino men. Many of the soldiers who were sent to Vietnam were younger than 20 years old.

As anti-war protests broke out across America, the US government received more pressure to withdraw. American soldiers left Vietnam on March 29, 1973, but by then almost 58,000 men had died or were missing in action.

> In April 1967, Martin gave his first public anti-war speech, "Beyond Vietnam," at the Riverside Church in New York. He had hoped to push leaders toward peace talks, but instead his anti-war speech caused him to lose many supporters. The Federal Bureau of Investigation (FBI) was particularly wary of him. They'd been monitoring him ever since the Montgomery bus

boycott and had even wiretapped Martin's home phone and listened in on his private conversations.

Over the years, Martin also mourned the deaths of many activists, including Medgar Evers, James Chaney, Andrew Goodman, and, of course, John F. Kennedy. He mourned, too, for Malcolm X, a civil rights leader who had a different approach to bringing about change. Martin and Malcolm X had met only once, on March 26, 1964, in Washington, DC, where they'd had a chance to speak briefly. Less than a year later, Malcolm X was assassinated.

Malcolm X

Malcolm Little was born on May 19, 1925, in Omaha, Nebraska. His childhood was full of hardship, and he spent time in foster care after his father was murdered by members of the KKK. But his life changed when he was sentenced to prison and introduced to the Nation of Islam, a black Muslim political movement.

The group's main belief is that black people are the original people, and that every other race came from them. Malcolm changed his last name from "Little" to "X" because he believed that "Little" was not his true lineage but rather was tied to the people who had kept his ancestors enslaved. He quickly rose within the leadership of the Nation of Islam and became one of the organization's best-known activists.

Malcolm was against the idea of integration and believed that violence should be met with violence. He was willing to defend himself by any means necessary. Although Malcolm X changed his views later in life and ultimately split from the Nation of Islam, he is best known for these radical approaches. After he was openly critical of their leader, Nation of Islam members fatally shot Malcolm X on February 21, 1965, at the Audubon Ballroom in Harlem in New York.

Martin continued to receive threats against his own life, but rather than go into hiding, he made the risks of activism a part of his teachings.

The road ahead is not altogether a smooth one. There are no broad highways that lead us easily and inevitably to quick solutions. But we must keep going.

LABOR RIGHTS IN MEMPHIS

In the spring of 1968, Martin's work led him to Memphis, Tennessee, where black city sanitation workers were fighting to earn the same wages as white workers.

Martin first visited Memphis in March 1968, to participate in a nonviolent protest with the black sanitation workers. But the march turned so violent that it had to be stopped halfway through. Martin hoped that when he returned in early April, he would be able to help the workers bring about the changes they desired.

On April 3, when Martin arrived again in Memphis, he gave another of his famous speeches, "I've Been to the Mountaintop," at Mason Temple Church of God in Christ. He encouraged the citizens of Memphis to use nonviolent protests to bring about the economic equality promised by the Civil Rights Act. Toward the end of his speech, Martin told those who had gathered: "We've got some difficult days ahead. But it really doesn't matter with me now, because I've been to the mountaintop.... And I've seen the Promised Land.... I want you to know tonight, that we, as a people, will get to the Promised Land. And so I'm happy tonight; I'm not worried about anything; I'm not fearing any man."

The next day, Martin and other members of the SCLC were at the Lorraine Motel preparing for an event later that evening. Whenever the men visited Memphis, they often stayed in the same room—room 306—and that's where they spent much of the day. Later, as they got ready for a private dinner at the home of Memphis minister Reverend Samuel "Billy" Kyles, Martin got dressed in one of his signature dark suits and put on a necktie.

At around 6:00 p.m., as his friends were finishing getting ready for dinner, Martin was standing alone on the balcony, as he had done countless times before, when a shot rang out.

Martin's friends heard the gunshot and rushed to see what had happened. They found him lying on the balcony, unconscious. Martin had been shot on the right side of his head. They looked around and saw a man running from a rooming house across the street, and they pointed in his direction in the hope that onlookers in the street below would help. An ambulance arrived quickly, and although Martin was rushed to St. Joseph's Hospital, where doctors tried to save his life, he died at 7:05 p.m.

After a thorough investigation and an intense manhunt, James Earl Ray would be arrested for the murder of one of America's greatest civil rights leaders.

Who Was James Earl Ray?

Born on March 10, 1928, in Alton, Illinois, James Earl Ray was an openly racist criminal. In early 1968, he started planning and gathering supplies to assassinate Martin Luther King Jr. After reading in the newspaper that Martin would be in Memphis in early April, James rented a room at a nearby hotel and waited for his opportunity. As Martin stepped out onto the balcony on the evening of April 4, 1968, James fired a single shot and killed him. After fleeing the scene and going into hiding, James was finally captured in March 1969. He confessed to the murder, which spared him from receiving the death penalty. He died in prison on April 23, 1998.

President Johnson was on his way to a Democratic fundraiser when he learned that Martin, a man he'd long admired and met with many times to discuss civil rights issues, had been assassinated. Like the rest of the nation, President Johnson was devastated. He issued Presidential Proclamation 3839, designating Sunday, April 7, 1968, as a day of national mourning.

> "I rarely have felt that sense of powerlessness more acutely than the day Martin Luther King Jr. was killed."
> —President Lyndon B. Johnson

As the public learned of Martin's untimely death, an outbreak of riots spread across America. Black people were angry that they'd lost one of the few men they trusted to advocate for their rights. In some cities, the violence and rioting were so bad that the National Guard had to be called in to restore order.

On April 9, 1968, thousands of well-wishers gathered outside Martin's home church in Atlanta, where his private memorial was being held. Inside Ebenezer Baptist Church, Coretta and Martin's children, along with other family members and close friends, bid their farewells to the man they'd loved, respected, and admired. And outside, so many people came to pay their respects that some even gathered on top of the church's roof and on neighboring rooftops. The city of Atlanta was covered in a veil of sadness. As civil rights activist Heather Booth said of Martin's death, "It was like the breaking of a dream, the breaking of our hopes."

Morehouse's president, Benjamin E. Mays, tearfully delivered Martin's eulogy. Years before, both men had promised to do this if one died before the other, and President Mays was heartbroken that Martin had died before him. Martin was only thirty-nine years old.

> "Here was a man who believed . . . that the pursuit of violence at any time is ethically and morally wrong . . . and that only love and forgiveness can break the vicious circle of revenge." —Benjamin E. Mays

A few days after Martin's funeral, on April 11, President Johnson signed the Fair Housing Act of 1968, which addressed one of Martin's wishes. It prohibited housing discrimination on the basis of race, religion, and national origin. People found comfort in knowing that even though Martin had died, his life's work resulted in laws that would advance the civil rights of black people and other minorities.

CONCLUSION

AN AMERICAN HERO

During the civil rights era, Martin's quest for equality took him around the world. He traveled more than six million miles, on planes, on trains, on boats, in cars, and on buses, to deliver over 2,500 speeches. A reporter once asked Martin why he traveled so much, especially to Southern states and cities, where he faced danger. He wanted to know why Martin didn't just make a phone call or write letters to keep himself safe. Martin famously said:

Injustice anywhere is a threat to justice everywhere.

Rather than stay in the comfort of his home, Martin chose to join with people on the ground. This was just one of many qualities that made him an American leader and hero.

A LASTING LEGACY

In his fight for civil rights, Martin was arrested and imprisoned dozens of times. Some of his actions were deliberate—he often knew that if he followed through on his nonviolent protests, he would be arrested. Other times, Martin was the victim of police harassment. Once, he was arrested and imprisoned for driving five miles over the speed limit.

Despite the many challenges and obstacles, Martin refused to let anything deter him from advancing the civil rights movement. In addition to being one of the youngest recipients of the Nobel Peace Prize, in 1964, Martin was posthumously awarded the Presidential Medal of Freedom in 1977 and a Congressional Gold Medal in 2004.

Martin also left a legacy at Morehouse College, where, in 1978, the Martin Luther King Jr. International Chapel was built to honor his legacy.

It is considered one of the world's most important religious memorials, housing over 150 paintings, figures, and exhibits featuring civil and human rights leaders, including the man who'd influenced King so much—Mohandas Gandhi. Since 1978, more than a million people have visited the Martin Luther King Jr. International Chapel.

Coretta Scott King made sure that Martin's legacy lived on through her own work, too. She and their children dedicated their lives to serving as advocates for human and civil rights around the world. Coretta was especially devoted to continuing the work she and Martin had discussed during their first date in 1952. Four days after Martin's assassination, Coretta flew to Memphis, where he had been killed, and led a march in his honor. In 1968, she assisted with the Poor People's Campaign that Martin had planned. Even as late as 1980, Coretta was arrested in Washington, DC, for protesting apartheid in South Africa.

In 1968, Coretta established the Martin Luther King Jr. Center for Nonviolent Social Change to commemorate her husband's dedication to the civil rights movement. In addition to containing the largest collection in the world of Martin's personal writings, the center allows visitors to listen to oral history interviews with Martin's family and friends and with other civil rights activists. The King Center is located right next door to Martin's former church, Ebenezer Baptist Church, in Atlanta, Georgia, and is visited by thousands of people every year.

> "I am indebted to my wife, Coretta, without whose love, sacrifices, and loyalty neither life nor work would bring fulfillment. She has given me words of consolation when I needed them and a well-ordered home where Christian love is a reality." —Martin Luther King Jr.

In the United States, there are approximately 730 streets named after Martin Luther King Jr. More than a thousand roadways around the world bear his name, including streets in Haiti, Germany, and France. And in honor of Martin's life, the Lorraine Motel is now the location of the National Civil Rights Museum. A wreath forever rests on the very spot where he was assassinated.

There is also the Martin Luther King Jr. Memorial in Washington, DC. It is located next to the National Mall, where Martin gave his historic "I Have a Dream" speech. The memorial includes the Stone of Hope—a granite statue of Martin.

And of course, Martin Luther King Jr. inspired many activists, politicians, and leaders, including the first black president of the United States.

"He started small, rallying others who believed their efforts mattered, pressing on through challenges and doubts to change our world for the better. A permanent inspiration for the rest of us to keep pushing towards justice."
—President Barack Obama

⋛ THE CONTINUED FIGHT ⋚

Following Martin's assassination, America took great strides in protecting the civil rights and freedoms of its citizens. In addition to President Johnson's signing of the Civil Rights Act of 1968, the Civil Rights Act of 1964 was expanded in 1991 to include protections for employees who sue for discrimination in the workplace.

It was no longer legal to keep black people out of schools, restaurants, or public places anywhere in the United States.

Even though America has made significant advances since the civil rights era thanks to Martin Luther King Jr., there is still work to be done. As long as injustice exists, it is everyone's responsibility to address it wherever and whenever we see it.

Timeline

African slaves arrive in Jamestown, Virginia.

September 22
President Abraham Lincoln issues the Emancipation Proclamation.

1619   1861   1862

April 12
The Civil War begins.

March 2
Claudette Colvin is arrested for refusing to give up her seat to a white passenger.

June 18
Martin and Coretta Scott are married.

1929 1953 1954 1955

January 15
Martin Luther King Jr. is born in Atlanta, Georgia.

May 17
The US Supreme Court issues its decision in *Brown v. Board of Education* declaring the segregation of public schools unconstitutional.

April 9
General Robert E. Lee, commander of the Confederate army, surrenders to Union army commander General Ulysses S. Grant in Virginia, signifying the end of the Civil War.

May 18
The US Supreme Court issues its ruling in *Plessy v. Ferguson* declaring that "separate but equal" facilities are constitutional.

1865

1896

December 18
The Thirteenth Amendment to the US Constitution, by which slavery is abolished, is formally adopted and goes into effect.

DON'T RIDE CITY BUSES

END SEGREGATION

August 31
Emmett Till's body is found in Mississippi's Tallahatchie River.

December 1
Rosa Parks is arrested.

November 17
Yolanda Denise, the Kings' first child, is born.

December 5
The Montgomery bus boycott begins. The Montgomery Improvement Association is formed and Martin is elected its president.

GROWTH AND PROGRESS

January 30
Martin's Montgomery home is bombed.

January 10–11
Martin is named chairman of the Southern Christian Leadership Conference.

1956   1957

November 13
The US Supreme Court rules that Alabama bus segregation laws are unconstitutional.

February 18
Martin appears on the cover of *Time* magazine.

October
Martin I the King second child, born.

January 31
Dexter Scott, the Kings' third child, is born.

March 28
Bernice Albertine, the Kings' fourth child is born.

1960 1961 1962 1963

October 19
Martin is arrested during a sit-in demonstration in Atlanta. He is released on October 27.

September 28
Martin is attacked by American Nazi Party member Roy James while in Birmingham, Alabama.

154

September 17
Stride Toward Freedom: The Montgomery Story is published.

February 3
Martin embarks on a monthlong visit to India.

February 1
Martin becomes the assistant pastor at Ebenezer Baptist Church in Atlanta.

1958   1959   1960

September 20
Izola Ware Curry stabs Martin in Harlem.

May 25—28
An all-white Montgomery jury finds Martin not guilty of tax fraud.

WE MARCH FOR JOBS

April 16
Martin writes "Letter from Birmingham Jail."

September 15
The 16th Street Baptist Church in Birmingham is bombed.

August 28
Martin delivers his "I Have a Dream" speech at the March on Washington for Jobs and Freedom.

November 22
President John F. Kennedy is assassinated.

SHARE CARS WITH YOUR FRIENDS

155

July 2
The Civil Rights Act of 1964 is passed.

March 7
Bloody Sunday takes place in Selma, Alabama.

1964　　1965

December 10
Martin receives the Nobel Peace Prize.

February 21
Malcolm X is assassinated.

August 6
The Voting Rights Act of 1965 is passed.

WE MARCH FOR JOBS

July 11
Martin is awarded the Presidential Medal of Freedom.

1977　　2004

Martin is awarded the Congressional Gold Medal.

WE DEMAND EQUAL RIGHTS NOW

GROWTH AND PROGRESS

January 26
Martin and Coretta move the family to Chicago, Illinois.

April 4
Martin is assassinated at the Lorraine Motel in Memphis, Tennessee.

1966   1968

April 3
Martin delivers his final speech, "I've Been to the Mountaintop."

April 11
The Civil Rights Act of 1968 is passed.

Further Reading

→ *I Am Martin Luther King, Jr.* (Ordinary People Change the World) by Brad Meltzer (Dial Books for Young Readers, 2016)

→ *Let the Children March* by Monica Clark-Robinson (HMH Books for Young Readers, 2018)

→ *Martin Rising: Requiem for a King* by Andrea Davis Pinkney (Scholastic, 2018)

→ *Young Civil Rights Heroes* (10 True Tales) by Allan Zullo (Scholastic, 2014)

Websites

→ brainpop.com/socialstudies
/famoushistoricalfigures/martinlutherkingjr
An animated educational website with
sections about the life of Martin Luther King
Jr. and the civil rights movement.

→ kinginstitute.stanford.edu
Information about Martin Luther King Jr.
and his legacy.

Glossary

abolition: The act of officially ending or stopping something; specifically, doing away with slavery.

advocate: A person who supports or promotes the interests of a cause or group.

Black Codes: Southern laws designed to restrict newly freed slaves' civil, constitutional, and labor rights.

boycott: Refusal to deal with a person, store, or organization until certain conditions are met.

citizenship: The status of being an inhabitant of a city, town, state, or country.

civil rights: The rights that every citizen has, especially the rights to be treated fairly and equally.

Confederate: Someone who fought for or supported Southern Confederate states in the Civil War, especially in regard to slavery.

Glossary

descendants: People who are related to a person or group of people who lived at an earlier time.

desegregation: The end of practices that enforce separation based on race, class, or ethnic group; see also *integration*.

discrimination: Treatment that unfairly causes harm to some individuals but not others.

harassment: Behavior that creates an unpleasant or hostile situation for another, especially using uninvited and unwelcome verbal or physical conduct.

hate group: An organization whose members have beliefs or practices that oppose people because of their race, religion, ethnicity, sexual orientation, or gender identity.

integration: The act of bringing two or more different groups together as equals; see also *desegregation*.

Glossary

Jim Crow laws: Late nineteenth-century and twentieth-century state and local laws that enforced racial segregation.

Ku Klux Klan: A hate group that was established by former Confederates after the Civil War. Members believe that white people are racially superior, and are known for intimidating, assaulting, or murdering people they believe are inferior or who oppose their views. Also known as the KKK and the Klan.

Negro: A dated and now sometimes offensive term for a member of a race native to Africa and classified according to physical features, such as dark skin.

segregation: The separation or isolation of a race, class, or ethnic group by residence in a restricted area, by separate facilities, or by other discriminatory means.

stereotype: A widely held but biased idea about a person, place, or thing.

Glossary

unconstitutional: Not consistent with the United States Constitution, which assures that US citizens have certain rights.

US Supreme Court: The highest federal court in the United States, whose nine justices have the power to hear and rule on all state and local court cases.

Index

A

Abernathy, Ralph David, 73, 75
abolition/abolitionists, 7, 9, 90
Alabama
   16th Street Baptist Church bombing, 118, 121, 155
   Birmingham, 97, 99–104, 107, 118, 154
   Bloody Sunday, 126–127, 128, 156
   Montgomery, 55–56, 58, 59, 60, 66–67, 73, 94, 127, 128
   Montgomery bus boycott, 67–70, 72, 76, 79, 83, 89, 131–132, 153–154
   Montgomery Improvement Association (MIA), 68, 72, 73, 81, 153
American Nazi Party, 97, 113, 154

B

Baptist religion/churches, 17, 26, 37, 41, 55, 73, 74, 83, 140, 146
   Dexter Avenue Baptist Church, 55, 61
   Ebenezer Baptist Church, 17, 26, 73, 83, 140, 146, 155
Barbour, J. Pius, 41, 43, 44
Big Six, the, 108–110, 111
Big Ten, the, 111, 113, 115, 117
Black Codes, 10
Black Lives Matter, 90
Booker T. Washington High School, 29–30
books and writings
   "Letter from Birmingham Jail," 101, 104, 155
   Stride Toward Freedom: The Montgomery Story, 80, 155
Boston University, 47–48, 53, 55
Bryant, Carolyn, 62

C

Chicago Freedom Movement, 129–130
Children's Crusade, 102–104
Civil Rights Acts, 121–122, 125, 130, 135, 142, 148, 156, 157
civil rights movement, 2, 4, 17, 54, 58–60, 72, 73, 75, 78, 79, 86

Index

88, 90, 99, 106, 107–108, 115, 120, 124, 144
Civil War, 8–9, 40, 112, 152–153
Colvin, Claudette, 60–61, 67, 72
Confederate army, 8–9, 90, 153
Connor, Eugene "Bull," 100, 102–103
Constitution, US, 9, 11, 30, 60
   Thirteenth Amendment, 9, 13
   Fourteenth Amendment, 11, 13, 110
   Fifteenth Amendment, 11
Cook, Samuel Dubois, 35
Crozer Theological Seminary, 40, 41–43, 45, 47
Curry, Izola Ware, 81, 155

D

David T. Howard Colored Elementary School, 25
Declaration of Independence, 4
Detroit, Michigan, 3
Douglass, Frederick, 37
DuBois, W. E. B., 58

E

Eisenhower, Dwight D., 77, 79–80
Emancipation Proclamation, 8

F

Faubus, Orval, 76
Federal Bureau of Investigation (FBI), 131
Finlayson, William E., 35
Freedom Rides, 86–87

G

Gandhi, Mohandas (Mahatma), 37, 38, 39, 45, 46, 81–82, 124, 145
Georgia
   Albany, 95–96
   Atlanta, 17, 19, 22, 23, 26, 28, 31, 34, 41, 49, 73, 83, 123, 140, 146, 155
   Sweet Auburn, 18, 19, 23

H

Historically Black Colleges, 31, 32, 46, 83
Howard University, 46

Index

I

indentured servants, 5–6

J

Jackson, Mahalia, 3, 79, 113

James, Roy, 97–98

Jamestown, Virginia, 5, 152

Jim Crow laws, 11, 12, 29, 57

Johnson, Lyndon B., 121, 126, 130, 139, 142, 148

Johnson, Mordecai, 46

K

Kennedy, John F., 92–93, 105, 106, 107, 110, 117, 119–120, 121, 132, 155

King, Alberta Williams, 17, 21, 24, 26, 28, 44, 51

King, Alfred Daniel, 17, 21

King, Bernice Albertine, 154

King, Coretta Scott, 49–52, 53, 55, 64, 71, 87, 123, 140, 145, 152, 157

King, Dexter Scott, 154

King, Martin Luther III, 87, 154

King, Willie Christine, 17, 21, 43

King, Yolanda Denise, 64–65, 71, 87, 153

King Sr., Martin Luther, 17, 19, 26, 27, 28, 51, 52, 83

Ku Klux Klan (KKK), 99–100, 113, 118, 133

L

Lincoln, Abraham, 8–9, 152

Lincoln Memorial, 2, 112

Little Rock Nine, 76–78

Luther, Martin, 27–28, 45

M

Malcolm X, 132–134, 156

March on Washington, 2, 4, 108, 109, 112–117, 118, 155

Martin Luther King Jr. Center for Nonviolent Social Change, 145–146

Martin Luther King Jr. International Chapel, 144–145

Martin Luther King Jr. Memorial, 147

Index

Mays, Benjamin E., 36, 37, 39, 45, 117, 141–142

Memphis, Tennessee, 135–137, 145
  Lorraine Motel, 136–137, 146
  Poor People's Campaign, 145
  National Civil Rights Museum, 146

Morehouse College, 31, 32, 33, 34, 35, 36, 39, 41, 144

National Association for the Advancement of Colored People (NAACP), 58–59, 66, 67, 70, 76, 78, 86, 95, 109

Newspapers/magazines/media, 29, 34, 52, 54, 89, 105, 107

Nixon, E. D., 6

Nobel Peace Prize, 123–125, 144, 156

O

Obama, Barack, 78, 124, 147

P

Parks, Rosa, 65–67, 153

Powell, Mary, 49, 51, 52

Prayer Pilgrimage for Freedom, 79

Prinz, Rabbi Joachim, 111, 115

R

Randolph, A. Philip, 109, 117

Ray, James Earl, 138

Reddick, Lawrence, 81

Robinson, Jo Ann, 67

S

segregation/desegregation, 4, 11–12, 13, 14, 23, 24, 29, 33, 47, 50, 53, 54, 59, 63, 65, 70–71, 72, 73, 75, 85, 86, 95–96, 99, 101, 107–108, 110, 118, 125, 152, 154

sit-ins
  Birmingham, 100, 102
  Greensboro, 84–86
  Atlanta, 91, 154

slavery, 4–7, 8, 12, 14, 24, 90

Southern Christian Leadership Conference (SCLC), 75, 76, 83, 89, 95, 97, 109, 126, 135

Index

speeches
  "Beyond Vietnam," 131
  "Give Us the Ballot," 79
  "I Have a Dream," 2–4, 116, 147, 155
  "I've Been to the Mountaintop," 135, 157
  "Normalcy—Never Again," 3
Student Nonviolent Coordinating Committee (SNCC), 86, 95, 109, 126
Supreme Court of the United States, 12, 13, 79, 86–87, 154
  Brown v. Board of Education, 53–53, 59, 152
  Gayle v. Browder, 72
  Plessy v. Ferguson, 12–13, 153

T
Thoreau, Henry David, 34
Thurman, Dean Howard, 48
Till, Emmett, 61–64, 67, 84, 153
Tulsa Race Massacre, 15

U
Underground Railroad, 7, 8, 40
Union army, 8–9

V
Vietnam War, 130–131
voting rights/voter suppression, 56–57, 125, 129, 156

W
Walker, Wyatt Tee, 3
Wallace, George, 99
Washington, Booker T., 37
Washington, DC, 2, 46, 79, 108, 110, 132, 145, 147
Wells-Barnett, Ida B., 58
Williams, Jennie Celeste Parks, 18, 19–20, 28
Williams, Reverend Adam Daniel, 18
Willie, Charles Vert, 35

Y
Yonge Street Elementary School, 22, 25

FOLLOW THE TRAIL!

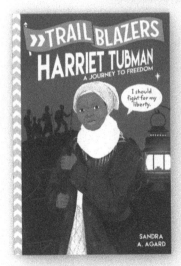

TURN THE PAGE FOR A SNEAK PEEK AT THESE TRAILBLAZERS BIOGRAPHIES!

Trailblazers: J. K. Rowling excerpt text copyright © 2020 by Cath Senker.
Illustrations copyright © 2020 by Tom Heard.
Cover art copyright © 2020 by Luisa Uribe.
Published in the United States by Random House Children's Books,
a division of Penguin Random House LLC, New York.

… TRAIL BLAZERS

J. K. ROWLING
BEHIND THE MAGIC

There is always room for a story.

CATH SENKER

The Swinging Sixties

The late 1960s were a time of considerable cultural change in the United Kingdom, the United States, and other countries. Bands such as the Beatles and the Rolling Stones were revolutionizing the music industry, and young people wore daring new fashions: brightly colored clothes, tiny miniskirts, and widely flared, or bell-bottom, jeans. Some people were inspired to become involved in social movements—for example, campaigning against nuclear weapons or against the US involvement in the Vietnam War. Even Joanne's parents, in their small village, were influenced by the new culture. They loved dancing to Beatles records in their living room.

AN IMAGINATIVE GIRL

Peter and Anne enjoyed reading, and their home was full of books. They always read to the girls at bedtime. Joanne especially loved fantasy and classic books. When she was four, she caught the measles and was stuck in bed for days. Her dad read Kenneth Grahame's *The Wind in the Willows* to her, with tales of the animal characters Rat, Mole, Toad, and Badger, who live in the English countryside and go on adventures.

THE WIZARDING WORLD

While Joanne was expanding her charitable work, Warner Bros. was seeking a way to extend the extraordinarily profitable world of Harry Potter once the final movie was released in 2011. In the United States, Universal Studios made an agreement with Warner Bros. to create a theme park.

The Wizarding World of Harry Potter opened in Orlando, Florida, in 2010. It re-creates the magical shops of Diagon Alley, offers underground journeys deep beneath Gringotts Bank, and takes visitors on roller-coaster rides into the Forbidden Forest to meet magical creatures.

Trailblazers: Stephen Hawking excerpt text copyright © 2020 by Alex Woolf.
Illustrations copyright © 2020 by David Shephard.
Cover art copyright © 2020 by Luisa Uribe.
Published in the United States by Random House Children's Books,
a division of Penguin Random House LLC, New York.

>>TRAIL BLAZERS
STEPHEN HAWKING
A LIFE BEYOND LIMITS

We can understand the universe.

ALEX WOOLF

A Theory of Everything

Quantum mechanics explains how the world works at the scale of the very small, while Einstein's theory of general relativity explains how the world works on the scale of the large. The trouble is, they describe what seem like two different universes. At large scales, gravity is the dominant force; in the quantum world, three other forces—electromagnetism and the strong and weak nuclear forces—hold sway. The great challenge of physics over the past century has been to find a "theory of everything," a set of laws that describe how the universe works at all scales.

≡ PRESENTING THE DISCOVERY ≡

Stephen told his colleagues about his discovery in January 1974. It caused huge excitement. His friend Martin Rees told Dennis Sciama: "Have you heard? Stephen's changed everything!" Roger Penrose phoned Stephen, who was just sitting down to his birthday dinner with family and guests. Penrose was so excited, he kept Stephen talking for ages, and the food got cold.

Stephen formally presented his idea at a conference in Oxford in February. It was met with a baffled silence. Many in the audience didn't understand Stephen's arguments. Those who did were shocked. How could anything come out of a black hole? The conference chairman, Professor John Taylor, eventually spoke up.

A UNIVERSE WITH NO BOUNDARIES

Stephen's research into the very early universe led him to some startling conclusions. In 1983, he published a paper with American physicist James Hartle describing what they termed the "no-boundary proposal." In this, they suggested that there might be no boundary—that is, no beginning or ending—to the universe. This was not to say that Stephen had lost faith in the big bang theory. What he was arguing was that scientists' whole understanding of the big bang was mistaken. In their paper, Hawking and Hartle asked readers to imagine traveling backward in time toward the very beginning of the universe.

THIS WAY TO **THE BIG BANG!**

As we approach the singularity that gave rise to the big bang, they wrote, everything becomes extremely compressed. It becomes so compressed that the differences between space and time disappear. Time becomes like another dimension of space. This is, of course, impossible for us to imagine with our human brains. Time isn't normally something we can see or touch—it's just the flow of events.

But what happens in the extremely early universe is that space and time merge to form something called four-dimensional space (you can't picture this, so don't even try!). This four-dimensional space curves around to become a closed surface, like a ball. A ball is not infinite in size, yet it has no edge or boundary, so anyone traveling across the ball's surface might think it were infinite.

And this, according to Hawking and Hartle, is how we should try to imagine the universe: not infinite, yet with no boundaries—no beginning or end.

Trailblazers: Harriet Tubman excerpt text copyright © 2019 by Sandra A. Agard.
Illustrations copyright © 2019 by Artful Doodlers.
Cover art copyright © 2019 by Luisa Uribe.
Published in the United States by Random House Children's Books,
a division of Penguin Random House LLC, New York.

≫TRAIL BLAZERS
HARRIET TUBMAN
A JOURNEY TO FREEDOM

I should fight for my liberty.

SANDRA A. AGARD

FAME AND FORTUNE

As she grew more famous, it became difficult for Harriet to make as many trips down South as before. Still desperate to help the Underground Railroad's efforts, in 1858 she began lecturing at locations all over the North. Her firsthand accounts of the Underground Railroad and its workings proved very popular, and she raised even more money to help fugitives, station masters, and conductors fighting to free slaves.

She was invited to speak in the parlor rooms of high society in Concord and Boston. In these anti-slavery speeches, Harriet told fascinating stories of her narrow escapes. Money poured in as more and more people heard about her amazing rescues.

HARRIET'S STORIES

One time, Harriet was traveling during the day in her home state of Maryland. She was wearing a large sunbonnet and kept her head bowed, but when she passed a former employer, Harriet worried that she would be recognized. Luckily, she'd just bought a couple of chickens at the market.

Thinking quickly, she opened the cage of chickens, which fluttered and squawked, causing an awful noise and diverting attention from herself.

On a different occasion, Harriet was traveling in a railroad car and noticed two gentlemen quietly discussing whether she was the woman on the Wanted poster at the station. Never one to panic, she simply picked up a newspaper and began to "read" it. Harriet Tubman was known to be illiterate—so this woman reading the paper studiously surely could not be the fugitive!

COMING SOON . . .

Amelia Earhart

Lin-Manuel Miranda